$7.95

DINING IN-HOUSTON

By Rona Abbott and Ann Criswell

Cover Photography by Dale Windham

PEANUT BUTTER PUBLISHING

Peanut Butter Towers   Seattle, Washington 98134

OTHER TITLES IN SERIES:
Dining In—Chicago
Dining In—Dallas
Dining In—Los Angeles
Dining In—Minneapolis/St. Paul
Dining In—Monterey Peninsula
Dining In—Philadelphia
Dining In—Pittsburgh
Dining In—Portland
Dining In—St. Louis
Dining In—San Francisco
Dining In—Seattle
Dining In—Toronto

Copyright © 1978 by Peanut Butter Publishing
First Printing August, 1978
Second Printing January, 1979
Third Printing October, 1979

ISBN 0-89716-019-3

CONTENTS

Introduction	iv
Arno's Italian Cuisine	1
Brennan's of Houston	11
The Brownstone	19
Charley's 517	29
Courtlandts	37
D'Amico's	45
Foulard's	57
Gaspair's	69
The Great Caruso	77
Harrigan's	85
Hebert's Ritz	95
Hugo's Window Box	103
La Quiche	111
Maxim's	123
Ninfa's	131
Ouisie's Table	139
The Rivoli	147
Rudi's	155
Ruggle's	163
Tivoli Inn	171
Tony's	179
Index	188

INTRODUCTION

When I first heard what was to be the title of this book, I was struck by the nuance involved in DINING IN—HOUSTON. As a native Houstonian (and amateur chef), I certainly recall that entertainment was generally centered around home "dining in" several decades ago. Only the few brave restaurateurs challenged this tradition, and had to be unique to survive the limited liquor laws, the excellence of Southern and Southwestern home cooking, and the infrequency of "dining out". Many of the early better restaurants were thus decorated like a home (Madeline's, The Green Parrot), or departed to a striking and theatrical ambiance (College Inn, Portofino's, The Red Lion) to imply a mood of entertainment away from the house.

Dining out in our city today, with the average Houstonian being twenty-seven years of age, is a much more frequent and youthful experience. Having become a truly cosmopolitan business and cultural center with a population which has doubled every decade since 1940, Houston has welcomed the ethnic elements who have migrated to the Southwest from all over the world, providing for not only a diverse demand but also a sumptuous abundance of international menus and cuisine.

Although I have sampled from the kitchens of most of the restaurants listed herein, fortunately, I was not given the difficult task of determining who would and would not be included in this book, for in excellence of service, taste, and freshness of recipe, as well as uniqueness of decor, there are far more eating establishments of worth than are compiled in this limited selection. Add to these the small "neighborhood favorites" in our spread-out city, and the challenge becomes even greater.

As the close recipient of the abundant yield in vegetables and citrus crops of the fertile Rio Grande Valley region, the fresh Gulf Coast seafood, and beef from almost adjacent ranches, Houston has an unrivaled opportunity to provide restaurants with "homegrown" resources for their preparations. Our tradition "under six flags" also makes for some unique recipes in these restaurants that have then our distinct character, and it is in this area that DINING IN—HOUSTON makes a real contribution to the vast lexicon of cookbooks. Each restaurant has been asked to select only *one* complete menu, and to share with us the ability to serve our friends and family those foods of which the restaurant feels most proud.

The explosion of interest in gourmet cooking and enjoyment of fine wines is one in which I've enjoyed being a part, and our richness of restaurants today helps reinforce this passion. Houstonians have long been intrigued with knowledge, and this book provides an excellent "how-to" from some of the best. So whether you use it to test the recommended menu at the restaurant, or to test their recipes *chez vous* with friends, I think you'll find DINING IN—HOUSTON a plan for taste delight. Enjoy!

Robert T. Sakowitz

Dinner for Four

Cheese-Stuffed Zucchini

Fettuccine with Pesto Sauce

Baked Flounder with Raisins, Pimiento and Almonds

Filetto Arno Supreme with Steamed Broccoli

Oven Baked New Potatoes

Lemon Mousse

Wine:

*With Zucchini, Fettuccine and Flounder—
Fazi-Battaglia Verdicchio*

*With Beef—Château St. Jean
Cabernet Sauvignon, 1974*

Janice Beeson and Michael Stein, Owners

Maria Campbell, Daytime Manager

Oscar Godie, Chef

"Some people wonder how we can have an Italian restaurant if we're not Italian," says Janice Beeson, co-owner of Arno's Italian Cuisine. "Those people always leave surprised at our authenticity."

Michael Stein and Janice Beeson opened Arno's in order to offer Houstonians food that is authentically Italian and nutritious. The restaurant has a homey atmosphere and it has been ranked as one of the city's best restaurants by Texas Monthly Magazine.

"We cook with fresh ingredients. We use few things that have dyes and preservatives and then only when there is no choice. Arno's is a healthful place to eat," adds Beeson. "Continually changing our menu is like opening a new restaurant everyday, but this gives us a chance to feature what is fresh. We also offer specialties, like kidneys, which you can't find elsewhere."

Both owners agree that it is important to know how to shop. "We spent the first year not only cooking, but finding better sources. A local fellow grows our herbs for us. He brings us whatever is fresh or we go to his yard and pick it ourselves. Adds Stein, "If we say it's fresh, it's fresh. If it's butter, it's butter, not margarine and if it's flounder or trout, it's *fresh* flounder or trout. I feel that the restaurant is a success because we're very honest with people."

5213 Cedar, Bellaire

ARNO'S ITALIAN CUISINE

CHEESE-STUFFED ZUCCHINI

Arno's makes bread crumbs from leftover French bread. Dry the bread in the oven, then grind or process in a food processor until a fine consistency.

2 medium zucchini squash
1/4 cup minced onion
1/8 cup fine bread crumbs
Salt and pepper to taste
2 tablespoons freshly grated Parmesan cheese
Fresh parsley

1. Wash zucchini and cut off ends. Drop into boiling water to cover for 10 minutes.
2. Drain and slice zucchini lengthwise. Scoop out pulp to make zucchini boats. Finely chop the pulp.
3. Sauté the onion in a small amount of butter until golden. Add zucchini pulp, bread crumbs, salt and pepper and 2 tablespoons of Parmesan cheese. Cook until soft and some of the moisture has evaporated.
4. Fill zucchini boats with mixture, dot with butter and sprinkle top with additional Parmesan cheese.
5. Bake in a hot (450-degree) oven until they are hot and the tops are golden. This will take about 10 to 15 minutes.
6. Sprinkle with chopped fresh parsley and serve.

ARNO'S ITALIAN CUISINE

FETTUCCINE WITH PESTO SAUCE

This makes more than a serving for four, but as long as you are going to the trouble of making handmade fettuccine, you might as well make an extra amount. To keep it fresh, spread the fettuccine out on a table to dry for a few hours, but do not let it dry out completely. Then toss and put it in plastic bags in the refrigerator. It will keep several days in the plastic bags if you toss it once every day and keep it refrigerated.

8 cups all-purpose flour
6 eggs
1 tablespoon salt
1½ cups water

1. Put the flour in a mound on a table or counter. Make a well in the middle and add the remaining ingredients which have been mixed together. Mix with hands until well combined. Knead until the dough springs back into shape, about 20 minutes.
2. On a lightly floured surface, divide into 10 to 12 pieces and roll each individually until very thin, like a crêpe.
3. Roll each strip of dough into a tube and slice into 1/2-inch wide pieces.
4. After they are all cut, gently unravel the small pieces, tossing them with your hands as if tossing a salad.
5. Spread out the tossed fettuccine on a table and let it dry for a few hours. Do not let it get crispy dry. Place in a plastic bag and refrigerate until time to cook.
6. To cook: Drop a generous handful of fettuccine per person into a pot of boiling salted water. Cook until *al dente* (still a little chewy, not mushy). Drain, toss with Pesto Sauce and serve immediately. *A serving only takes about 45 seconds to cook.*

ARNO'S ITALIAN CUISINE

PESTO SAUCE

We use a very good, smooth and light-tasting Spanish olive oil. If you like a slightly nuttier flavor, toast the pine nuts in the oven before using. Watch them carefully so they don't burn. The mixture will keep in the refrigerator for a long time.

1 cup chopped fresh basil leaves (no flowers)
3 or 4 tablespoons pignolia (pine nuts)
5 tablespoons grated fresh imported Parmesan cheese
3 garlic cloves, chopped
8 tablespoons imported olive oil
Salt to taste

1. Blend all the ingredients in an electric blender until smooth.
2. To serve, toss with freshly cooked *al dente* fettuccine. Serve immediately, topped with additional freshly grated Parmesan cheese.

***It's more important to know *why* things work instead of just the proper amounts of ingredients. If you know why things work, what to use and when to use it, amounts can be figured out.

Take a good cookbook like *Joy of Cooking* or Julia Child's book and instead of reading the recipes, read the preface to the section and the material between the recipes.***

ARNO'S ITALIAN CUISINE

BAKED FLOUNDER WITH RAISINS, PINE NUTS AND ALMONDS

If you can't find pine nuts, just increase the amount of almonds used. Be sure to use clarified butter. Here's an easy way to do it: Melt the butter and then set it in the refrigerator until it is chilled enough so that the butter has risen firmly to the top. Remove from pan and discard sediment.

4 fresh flounder filets (preferably the belly)
Clarified butter
Salt and pepper
Squeeze of fresh lemon juice
Golden raisins
Pine nuts (Pignolia)
Sliced almonds sautéed in a small amount of butter

1. Arrange the flounder filets in a pan. Brush them with clarified butter. Add a bit of salt and pepper and squeeze fresh lemon juice over them.
2. Bake at 400 degrees until done, about 12 to 15 minutes. They should be firm to the touch yet flake easily with a fork.
3. Top with equal amounts of golden raisins, pine nuts and sliced almonds, about 1/3 cup each (1 cup for four servings in all). Almonds should be sautéed in a small amount of butter until a pale gold color.

ARNO'S ITALIAN CUISINE

STEAMED BROCCOLI

At Arno's we like vegetables fresh and barely cooked so they're still really crunchy. Some people think that it's a mistake—that they haven't been cooked at all—but people who really like vegetables like them this way. In the restaurant, we parboil the broccoli about three minutes. It's then heated another minute or so before serving, but at home you could do it about four minutes in all.

1 large bunch broccoli
Melted butter
Fresh lemon juice
Salt and pepper

1. Cut broccoli into quarters and drop into boiling, salted water. Cook for about 4 minutes.
2. Serve with melted butter seasoned with salt, pepper and fresh lemon juice.

OVEN BAKED NEW POTATOES

Spanish olive oil
1 pound new potatoes, quartered
Salt and pepper
Fresh rosemary leaves

1. Coat a baking pan with olive oil. Spread new potatoes over pan and toss lightly with salt, pepper and fresh rosemary.
2. Bake at 375 degrees until potatoes are soft, about 20 minutes. Toss once or twice during cooking.

ARNO'S ITALIAN CUISINE

FILETTO ARNO SUPREME

4 (4 to 6-ounce) beef filets
Salt and pepper
4 slices unpeeled eggplant
2 or 3 thin slices onion
4 thin slices prosciutto
4 thin slices mozzarella cheese

1. Broil the filets on one side, season and turn; broil opposite side.
2. Pan-fry eggplant slices, then onion slices, in a small amount of olive oil.
3. Top filets with a slice of eggplant, a slice of prosciutto, a slice of mozzarella and onion.
4. Place in a hot (450 degrees) oven long enough for the cheese to melt.

If I were going to tell someone how to learn to cook, I would recommend getting Gourmet magazine for a year and just reading the back pages, 'The Final Touch', where it tells all about one kind of sauce stocks and basic things like that.

LEMON MOUSSE

We use very little sugar in desserts at Arno's and often experiment with recipes to see how much sugar can be deleted and still have it taste good. This dessert should be on the tart side.

2 teaspoons unflavored gelatin
2 tablespoons white wine or vermouth
1/3 cup fresh lemon juice
1½ tablespoons grated lemon rind
3 eggs, separated, plus 1 egg white
Sugar
1 cup heavy cream, whipped
Slices of lemon or fresh mint for garnish (optional)

1. Sprinkle gelatin over wine in a bowl and let soften 5 minutes. Add lemon juice and rind and stir the mixture over hot water until the gelatin is dissolved.
2. In a separate bowl, beat egg yolks with 2 tablespoons sugar. Gradually beat in the gelatin mixture.
3. In another bowl, beat 4 egg whites until foamy, then add 1/3 cup sugar and beat until it holds soft peaks.
4. Combine whipped cream with the egg yolk mixture. Fold in one-fourth of the egg white mixture. Add the cream mixture to the egg whites and fold gently until combined.
5. Spoon into stemmed glasses and chill for several hours. Garnish as desired. This can serve 4 to 6, depending on the size of the glasses.

Dinner for Six

Creole Turtle Soup au Sherry

Jill Jackson Salad

Trout With Roasted Pecans

Veal Kottwitz

Brennan's Bread Pudding with Whiskey Sauce

Wine:

With Soup, Salad and Trout — Pouilly Fuissé, 1973 or 1974, or California Riesling

With Veal — Beaujolais Julius Wile, or Château Figeac, 1974

With Dessert — Ockfener Bockstein, 1973

Ella, Adelaide, Dick and John Brennan, Owners

Noel Hennebery, General Manager

Hans Korrodi, Chef

Breakfasts and dinners at Brennan's are as much of a tradition in Houston as they are in New Orleans. Brennan's of Houston opened eleven years ago in the former Junior League building, a landmark building designed by John Staub, the city's renowned architect.

The Brennans brought their distinctive French-Creole cuisine to Houston and asked New Orleans architect August Perez to give their new restaurant a New Orleans character. The restaurant now is owned by the first generation Brennan family, and has a homelike atmosphere created by fabric-covered walls and draperies, antiques and cool brick walkways. The porch and balconies overlook a lush patio with splashing fountains. Thousands of Houstonians know the charm of having cocktails there. The Wine Room is popular for parties, and Jazz Brunch on Saturdays is a new favorite.

Well known menu items, such as Shrimp Remoulade, Pompano Pontchartrain and Bananas Foster, which Brennan's introduced to the world, vie with new dishes which are constantly added to the menu.

3300 Smith Street

CREOLE TURTLE SOUP AU SHERRY

1 cup butter
3 cups white onion, chopped
2 cups celery, chopped
1 cup flour
1/2 cup tomato purée
10 cups Turtle Stock (see below)
1 cup sherry
1/4 cup Worcestershire sauce
1½ pounds turtle meat (from Stock recipe)
3 hard-cooked eggs, finely chopped
1 cup fresh parsley, finely chopped
1 lemon, thinly sliced

1. In a soup kettle, melt the butter over medium heat. Add onion and celery and sauté until transparent.
2. Stir in flour and cook until browned.
3. Add the tomato purée and cook for 5 minutes more.
4. Add stock, sherry and Worcestershire sauce. Continue to cook slowly for 15 more minutes. Add turtle meat, prepared for stock recipe below, and egg. Simmer for 10 to 15 minutes. Remove from heat.
5. Stir in parsley and lemon slices. Serve at once.

TURTLE STOCK

Turtle meat is available at selected seafood markets occasionally, and sometime Brennan's, which usually gets its supply from New Orleans and will sell it to customers.

1½ pounds turtle meat
3 quarts water
2 bay leaves
2 teaspoons cayenne pepper
2 tablespoons salt

1. In a large kettle, cover turtle meat with water and add bay leaves, cayenne and salt.
2. Bring to a boil and cook until turtle meat is tender. Add more water if needed to keep liquid at about 2 quarts. Strain and reserve stock. Cut the meat into small cubes and use as above.

BRENNAN'S

JILL JACKSON SALAD

6 romaine lettuce leaves
1 large head iceberg lettuce
1/2 cup chopped hard-cooked eggs
1/2 cup bacon bits
Crumbled blue cheese
Sharp French Dressing
Artichoke hearts, sliced tomatoes, or sliced avocados (garnish)

1. Toss all ingredients well in a large salad bowl.
2. Pour in the dressing.
3. Serve on chilled plates, garnished, if desired, with artichoke hearts, sliced tomatoes or sliced avocados.

This salad is named for a *Times-Picayune* newspaper columnist in New Orleans.

TROUT WITH ROASTED PECANS

1 cup chopped pecans
3 ounces butter
Juice of 1 lemon
1 teaspoon Worcestershire sauce
6 trout filets
Flour
Butter
Lemon Butter Sauce (see Veal Kottwitz recipe)

1. Purée pecans with butter, lemon juice and Worcestershire sauce.
2. Season and lightly flour filets of trout. Pan sauté in butter.
3. Spread the pecan butter over fish and sprinkle with extra pecans. Top with 1 teaspoon Lemon Butter Sauce and place in the oven until pecans start to brown.
4. Serve immediately.

A Creole version of Trout Almondine, the pecans are appropriate for Texas since that is our state tree. The recipe comes from chef Paul Prudhomme of our New Orleans restaurant Commander's Palace.

VEAL KOTTWITZ

12 (2½-ounce) prime white veal filets (about 2 pounds veal)
Seasoned flour
1 pound mushrooms, sliced
1 pound artichoke bottoms
Lemon Butter Sauce

1. Pound veal until flat and thin. Dredge in seasoned flour and sear in oil in a large hot skillet for about 1 minute on each side, or until cooked. When ready, place on a plate.
2. In a pan, sauté mushrooms with a little butter; add artichoke bottoms and Lemon Butter Sauce and keep warm.
3. Spoon sauce over veal and serve.

LEMON BUTTER SAUCE

This sauce must be kept at room temperature and served within a few hours. The butter must be at room temperature, *not melted*, when it is added. The sauce also is used to top the Trout with Roasted Pecans.

Juice of 1 lemon
1/4 cup demi-glaze or brown sauce
1/2 teaspoon Worcestershire sauce
2 cups butter

1. Mix lemon juice, brown sauce and Worcestershire sauce in a pot and bring to a boil.
2. After boiling, cook at moderate heat and add butter slowly, stirring continuously with a wire whip. Season to taste.
3. Remove from heat.

BRENNAN'S

BRENNAN'S BREAD PUDDING WITH WHISKEY SAUCE

8 slices day-old bread, broken into pieces
3 cups scalded milk
1/2 cup cream
4 eggs
1/2 cup brown sugar
1 teaspoon vanilla
1/2 teaspoon cinnamon
Dash of nutmeg
1/4 cup butter
1/4 cup seedless raisins
1/4 cup whole pecans
Whiskey Sauce (see below)

1. Combine bread, milk and cream.
2. Beat eggs; add sugar and mix well.
3. Stir in the bread mixture and add vanilla, cinnamon and nutmeg.
4. Stir in the butter, raisins and pecans.
5. Pour into a buttered 2-quart baking dish and set in pan of warm water about 1 inch deep. Bake in a 350-degree oven for 1 hour or until a knife, inserted in center, comes out clean.

Bread pudding was originally created to make thrifty use of leftovers. We use stale French bread, heavy cream and light brown sugar.

WHISKEY SAUCE

3 egg yolks
1 cup sugar
1 teaspoon vanilla
1½ cups milk
1 tablespoon cornstarch
1/4 cup water
1½ ounces brandy

1. In a saucepan, slightly beat egg yolks. Add sugar, vanilla and milk and blend well. Cook over low heat until mixture comes to a boil.
2. Blend cornstarch in water and stir it into the hot mixture. Continue cooking until mixture thickens.
3. Remove from heat and stir in brandy. Serve when cooled.

Dinner for Four

Artichokes Brownstone with Sauce Louis

Avocado Velvet Soup

Brownstone Salad with Celery Seed Dressing

Beef Wellington with Sauce Perigourdine

Dante Silk Pie

Wine:

*With Artichokes, Soup and Salad —
Dry Creek Chardonnay, 1976*

*With Beef Wellington — Château Talbot
St. Julien, 1970*

*After Dessert — Warre's Vintage Port,
Frank Schoonmaker Selection, 1966*

Beau Theriot, Owner

Dean Allen and Carmen Campos, Chefs

The Brownstone was opened in 1973 by two friends who decided that they wanted a new and exciting challenge, completely different from their jobs of selling fine furniture and carpets to interior designers.

While on a trip to New Orleans, they began to collect the antique glasses and chairs that now furnish this restaurant. "We thought these glasses would be pretty in a restaurant," says Beau Theriot, now sole owner. "I charged over $1,000 worth of glasses on my American Express card. Then we saw the chairs and agreed that we had to open something." The "something" became a combination restaurant and antique gallery, opened in an old building, actually a lofty old garage, they had seen on the fringe of the River Oaks area.

"We opened, appealing to a special market—to the person who doesn't want the ordinary," adds Theriot. "We wanted to have the best of everything—the best food, the best service, the best atmosphere. Most places fall short of one of those. We were interested in offering creative gourmet cooking; something pleasing to the eye and very tasteful.

"We're always changing. So many places start off with a bang and then people think they can loosen up. Well, as things get better, I just tighten up. The better it gets, the better I have to make it."

"People don't come just to have dinner here; they come to spend an evening." It may be for dinner in the beautiful dining room with tented paisley ceiling and bronze Lalique chandelier, lunch in the Aviary, a garden room facing the New Orleans style courtyard or a reception in the French-styled Renaissance Room, which is dominated by a magnificent seven and one-half foot long English grand piano made in 1850. In the evening, guests may stop for drinks in the cocktail bar or Beau's Club Brownstone upstairs which offers a small dance floor, backgammon room and lounge area. Another recent addition is the wine room downstairs which seats twelve for small luncheons or tasting parties.

"We want people to have the feeling that this is a home, and that they have been invited to dinner. The Brownstone is the best of the things that life has to offer."

2736 Virginia

THE BROWNSTONE

ARTICHOKES BROWNSTONE WITH SAUCE LOUIS

Cook fresh artichokes by your favorite method. Staff member Carmen Campos, who is Columbian, says the best way to do them is in clay pots.

8 fresh artichoke bottoms
8 ounces fresh king crab meat
Juice of 1/2 lemon
Salt and white pepper
Sauce Louis (see below)

1. Mix crab, lemon juice and salt and pepper and stuff artichoke bottoms. Serve with Sauce Louis on top.

SAUCE LOUIS

1 cup mayonnaise
1/4 cup tomato sauce
2 hard-cooked eggs
2 tablespoons chopped fresh green onions
2 tablespoons chopped fresh parsley
1/4 cup heavy cream
1 small clove garlic, minced
Juice of 1/2 lemon
Salt and pepper to taste

1. Mix all ingredients and serve over stuffed artichokes.

THE BROWNSTONE

AVOCADO VELVET SOUP

This is one of our most popular soups. Since it contains no cream, it's light and has fewer calories. It's very refreshing on a hot day.

2 fresh avocados, pitted and peeled
3 cups chicken stock (preferably homemade)
1 tablespoon chopped green onions
Juice of 1/2 lime
Few drops Tabasco sauce
Salt and white pepper to taste
Sour cream and red caviar for garnish

1. Mix mashed avocados, stock and seasonings.
2. Blend and chill.
3. Garnish each bowl with a dollop of sour cream and red caviar.

THE BROWNSTONE

BROWNSTONE SALAD WITH CELERY SEED DRESSING

1 to 1½ pounds fresh spinach, torn into bite-sized pieces
4 to 6 slices bacon, cooked and crumbled
Grated Swiss cheese
Fresh sliced mushrooms, about 1¼ cups
Chopped fresh parsley
Dressing (see below)

1. Arrange spinach on a cold plate and top with bacon, cheese, mushrooms and parsley. Serve with dressing.

CELERY SEED DRESSING

2 egg yolks
1 tablespoon Dijon mustard
1 cup oil
1 cup sour cream
2 tablespoons diced green onion
1 tablespoon celery seed
1 teaspoon Worcestershire sauce
1 teaspoon white wine vinegar
Salt and white pepper

1. Whip egg yolks and mustard.
2. Add oil slowly to make a mayonnaise.
3. Add sour cream and mix with remaining ingredients. Store any remaining dressing tightly covered in refrigerator.

THE BROWNSTONE

BEEF WELLINGTON WITH SAUCE PERIGOURDINE

The Brownstone was the first restaurant in the South to serve individual Beef Wellington. When cooking this at home, remember that the beef should have a good bright color and feel like soft butter when you touch it. Clean and trim it well. The bread crumbs are made by grinding fresh French bread. Puff pastry dough is sometimes available from bakery shops, if you don't want to make your own.

2 pounds beef tenderloin, cleaned and trimmed
2 tablespoons onion, finely chopped
2 cups fresh mushrooms, finely chopped
Butter
Salt and pepper to taste
2 ounces dry sherry
1/2 cup freshly ground bread crumbs (from French bread)
6 ounces pâté de foie gras (homemade or canned)
Puff pastry dough (use your favorite basic recipe)
Egg wash (mix an egg with a little milk)

1. Brown meat. Let cool.
2. Sauté onions and mushrooms, seasoned with salt and pepper, in butter. Add sherry and simmer for a few minutes.
3. Add enough bread crumbs to absorb the juice; cool.
4. Spread pâté over the meat to cover. Cover the pâté with the mushroom mixture.
5. Roll puff pastry dough to about 1/8-inch thick. Cut 2 (10-inch) pieces. Place meat in the center of one square and cover with the other.
6. Seal with an egg wash. Trim dough to make an oval shape. Brush the whole Wellington with the egg wash to allow it to brown nicely.
7. Bake at 375 degrees for 30 minutes. Let rest 5 to 10 minutes before carving. Serve with Sauce Perigourdine.

SAUCE PERIGOURDINE

2 truffles
5 shallots, chopped.
1/4 cup Madeira wine
2 cups Espagnole Sauce, or basic brown sauce with a little tomato paste added

1. Slice truffles.
2. Sauté shallots and add Madeira; simmer until liquid is reduced by half.
3. Add to Espagnole Sauce and add essence of truffles. Simmer slowly for 30 minutes.
4. Add sliced truffles and serve with the Beef Wellington.

THE BROWNSTONE

DANTE SILK PIE

This is wonderful to keep in the freezer. Just take it out about fifteen minutes before you want to serve it. Baking the crust helps keep it from getting soggy.

1½ cups graham cracker crumbs
1/4 cup soft butter
1/3 cup sugar

1. Mix crumbs, butter and sugar until well blended. Press firmly against the bottom and sides of a 10-inch glass pie plate.
2. Bake at 375 degrees until golden brown, about 7 minutes. Cool.

THE BROWNSTONE

FILLING

1 cup half and half
1/2 cup sugar
6 ounces semisweet chocolate
6 egg yolks
2 tablespoons strong coffee
3 tablespoons dark crème de cacao
1/3 cup cognac
3 ounces miniature marshmallows

1. In the top of a double boiler, combine half and half, sugar and chocolate, and heat until the chocolate is melted.
2. Add the egg yolks, coffee, crème de cacao, cognac and marshmallows.
3. Cook until the marshmallows are melted and the mixture looks shiny.
4. Fill the pie shell and freeze for 4 to 6 hours.
5. Remove from freezer about 15 minutes before serving. Garnish with whipped cream, shaved chocolate or chocolate sauce and mint leaves.

Charley's 517

Dinner for Six

Charley's Shrimp Scampi

Cream of Broccoli Soup

Redfish à la Louisiana

Tournedos James

Spinach Soufflé

Charley's Strawberries Romanoff

Wine:

With Scampi—Les Petites Charron Meursault, Ropiteau, 1973

With Redfish—Chassagne-Montrachet, Frank Schoonmaker selection, 1973 or 1975

With Tournedos—Margaux or St. Julien, 1970

General Leisure Corporation, Owner

James Henderson, Manager

Curtis Calhoun, Chef

Charley's 517 plays many roles. It is a popular spot for downtown business luncheons and it does a brisk before and after-theater business because of its key location close to the Alley Theatre, Jones Hall for the Performing Arts, the Music Hall, and Civic Center. Charley's 517 also appeals to the fine dining, candlelight-and-wine set. Continental specialties head the menu, and there is much emphasis on seafood and veal.

"The restaurant combines a little bit of New Orleans and New York," says manager James Henderson. The muted decor is a mix of brick walls and arches, subtly colored furnishings, an intimate wine room and walls hung with framed historical newspaper pages, theater, symphony, ballet, opera and musical programs. A pianist plays for customers in the bar and dining room.

Henderson and chef Curtis Calhoun have worked their way through the ranks of several of Houston's finest restaurants, including the now defunct Portofino's, and several clubs. They previously worked together at Lakeside Country Club and Calhoun was at Houston Country Club during the tenure of the late Helen Corbitt.

Says Henderson, "We opened Charley's 517 in 1970, and we continue to strive to offer personal professional service and the best that money can buy."

517 Louisiana

CHARLEY'S SHRIMP SCAMPI

1 pound butter
2 large cloves garlic
Salt to taste
1 teaspoon white pepper
2 lemons
1½ cups good dry sherry such as Tio Pepe
1 tablespoon Worcestershire sauce
1/2 cup fresh parsley, finely chopped
24 to 30 extra large shrimp (10 to 12 count/pound)
1/4 cup glaze (Basic Brown Sauce)

1. Let butter come to room temperature. Mince the fresh garlic cloves. Put the butter, garlic, salt, pepper, the juice of 1 lemon, 1/2 cup sherry, Worcestershire sauce and 1/4 cup chopped parsley in a mixer at medium speed and whip until light and fluffy. Set aside.
2. Peel and devein shrimp, leaving the tails. Arrange shrimp in one saucepan.
3. In another saucepan, heat the butter, glaze and remaining sherry, stirring constantly until the mixture comes to a boil.
4. Add juice of the remaining lemon to the pan with the shrimp and place over heat. When shrimp pan is hot, add the butter mixture and let simmer for about 5 to 7 minutes, until the shrimp turns red. *Do not overcook*.
5. Serve in individual dishes and sprinkle with remaining chopped parsley. Serve with hot French bread.

To follow a recipe is one thing, but adding your own personal touches perfects it; that's what professionals do.

CREAM OF BROCCOLI SOUP

1 pound fresh broccoli, trimmed and divided into sections
3/4 cup butter
4 tablespoons flour
1 pint heavy cream
1/2 teaspoon salt
1/2 teaspoon white pepper
1/4 teaspoon A-1 Sauce
2 chicken bouillon cubes

1. Cook the broccoli in boiling salted water until about half done.
2. Remove from heat. Drain well, reserving liquid, and chop the broccoli into small pieces. Set aside.
3. Melt the butter in a saucepan. Add flour and cook for about 5 minutes over low heat. Do not brown.
4. Heat the cream and add it to the flour mixture, stirring well. Add liquid from broccoli and stir until smooth.
5. Add salt, pepper, A-1 Sauce and crushed bouillon cubes.
6. Simmer for about 20 minutes over very low heat. If soup is too thick, add a little heavy cream.

A good stock and sauce are the basis for success in cooking at home. Our sauces are made fresh in the kitchen and our Hollandaise sauce is made twice a day. One of the big problems with cooking at home is that you don't have the sauces already made and at hand. They take a lot of time and preparation. I've noticed in the last few years that people tend to substitute bouillon cubes for stock or to substitute canned soup for a good sauce. That alters the taste of the food. Our broccoli soup calls for chicken bouillon cubes which is acceptable since the cubes are used as a seasoning rather than as a liquid or stock.

REDFISH À LA LOUISIANA

1/2 cup fresh mushrooms, sliced
1 teaspoon chives
1 tablespoon chopped pimento
4 tablespoons butter
8 ounces lobster meat
1 quart half and half
Salt and pepper to taste
1/4 cup very dry sherry
4 (8-ounce) redfish filets, floured
Lemon wedges and parsley for garnish

1. Sauté the mushrooms, chives and pimento in butter with the lobster until tender.
2. Heat half and half in a separate pan.
3. Add flour to the lobster mixture and cook for 5 minutes. Do not brown.
4. Add hot half and half and stir until you have a medium sauce. Add salt and pepper. Add sherry and simmer over low heat until ready to serve.
5. Saute well-floured redfish filets in oil until golden brown. Drain. Serve with lobster sauce and garnish with lemon wedges and parsley.

Our restaurant is a little bit of Louisiana and New York, as shown in this recipe.

CHARLEY'S 517

TOURNEDOS JAMES

1 whole beef tenderloin, skinned and completely trimmed
1 cup clarified butter
3 ounces brandy
6 whole large white mushroom caps
1/3 cup flour
3/4 cup medium dry sherry
1 teaspoon white pepper and salt to taste
Squeeze of lemon juice
3 cups heavy cream
2 tablespoons chopped chives (may be freeze dried)
3 tablespoons chopped fresh parsley

1. Slice the tenderloin into 1-inch thick medallions. Salt and sauté in 2/3 cup clarified butter, over low heat, until rare to medium rare.
2. Add brandy and flambé. Remove meat from saucepan.
3. Sauté the mushroom caps until seared on both sides. Remove.
4. Mix flour with remaining butter and add the mixture to the pan. Cook over low heat, stirring constantly with a wire whip.
5. Add sherry, salt and pepper, and a squeeze of lemon. Continue stirring over low heat until the mixture is smooth. Add cream and chives and whip until light and smooth.
6. Arrange 2 medallions on each plate and top with one mushroom cap; add sauce.
7. Sprinkle with chopped parsley, garnish with fresh watercress, and serve.

Beef Tournedos James is one of the many menu specialties which we do at the table.

SPINACH SOUFFLÉ

1 pound fresh spinach, washed and chopped
1 cup bechamel sauce
1/4 teaspoon nutmeg
1/4 teaspoon salt
1/4 teaspoon white pepper
4 whole eggs
1 cup egg whites (about 8 large)
1/2 teaspoon cream of tartar

1. Preheat oven to 325 degrees. Grease a 2-quart casserole or soufflé dish.
2. Boil the spinach with only the water clinging to the leaves after it is washed. Drain and chop very well. Drain again.
3. Put the spinach in a mixing bowl and add the Bechamel sauce, nutmeg, salt and pepper. Stir.
4. In separate bowl, beat the eggs. Stir in the spinach mixture.
5. Beat the egg whites with cream of tartar in a separate bowl, using clean beaters. Fold the egg whites into the spinach mixture.
6. Turn into a prepared soufflé dish and bake for 35 to 45 minutes at 325 degrees. Serve immediately.

CHARLEY'S STRAWBERRIES ROMANOFF

This is our own special version. Remember to chill bowl, beaters, and cream thoroughly for best results.

2 cups heavy cream for whipping
3 tablespoons powdered sugar
2 or 3 drops fresh lemon juice
6 ounces Grand Marnier liqueur
3 cups fresh strawberries; washed, hulled and thinly sliced
1 quart vanilla ice cream
Whole strawberries for garnish

1. In cold metal bowl, beat the cream until it peaks. Beat in the powdered sugar and lemon juice (add a pinch of salt if desired).
2. Add 5 of the 6 ounces of Grand Marnier and the strawberries.
3. Break the ice cream into small pieces with a knife or spoon and fold it into the mixture.
4. Serve in frozen glasses or dessert dishes.
5. Top each dessert with one whole strawberry and part of the remaining Grand Marnier.

***The secrets to fine cooking are to follow recipes carefully and to use *fresh* ingredients. For example, if a recipe calls for mushrooms, use fresh, not canned, mushrooms.

Dinner for Four

Singing Shrimp

*Fresh Spinach Salad with
Burgundy Dressing*

Steak with Artichokes and Sour Cream

Broccoli with Lemon Butter

Crêpes Romanoff

Wine:

With Shrimp — Chassagne-Montrachet, 1975
With Steak — Château Lascombes, 1973
With Crêpes — Mumm's Cordon Rouge Brut

Jerry Daniel and Sandy Smith, Owners
John Kimble, Chef

Courtlandts is a sophisticated mixture of Old World opulence and New Orleans atmosphere. Its designer, Don Bolen, has blended cypress paneling salvaged from a New Orleans mansion, French Victorian gaslight chandeliers from an old Corpus Christi hotel, and leaded glass windows from a 19th century St. Louis residence, together with heavy draperies, mirrored columns and sconces for luxurious and dignified surroundings.

Bacchus, the symbol of the restaurant, overlooks the New Orleans-style courtyard and the bar, and appears on match and menu covers. The Wine Cellar, setting for intimate gourmet dinners, seats twelve. The table is set with Wedgwood, crystal and sterling that owner Sandy Smith bought from Patrick Dennis of "Auntie Mame" fame, a former Houston resident.

Courtlandts' principal owners were in the real estate business, and originally were looking for a tenant to open a restaurant in one of their buildings. Unable to find a tenant, they decided to open the restaurant themselves. In 1974, they doubled its size, adding private dining rooms, the wine cellar, patio, and Garden Dining Room.

Initially known as a prime rib and fine beef house, Courtlandts is evolving into a Continental restaurant with a menu that includes veal, fresh seafood and flambé dishes.

"Houston is very cosmopolitan," says Sandy Smith. "People here from other areas have taught us a lot about dining."

Courtlandts has received the Mobil Award and the Hospitality Magazine's "Top of the Table" Award.

611 Stuart

SINGING SHRIMP

4 tablespoons butter
2 teaspoons crushed garlic
2 teaspoons chopped chives
16 shrimp, shelled and deveined
1/2 cup (8 tablespoons) lump crab meat, chopped
1½ ounces dry vermouth
Juice of 1 lemon
Parsley and lemon wedges (garnish)

1. Melt butter in a large skillet over medium heat.
2. Add garlic, chives, shrimp, crab, vermouth and lemon juice.
3. Cook until the shrimp are done, about 4 minutes.
4. Serve in small dishes with lemon wedge and parsley garnish.

This dish is named for our waiter, Al Greene, who created the recipe and who always would sing quietly as he prepared it in the dining room.

COURTLANDTS

SPINACH SALAD WITH BURGUNDY DRESSING

The dressing is what makes this salad unique. We have tested it in various amounts and have found that it must be prepared in one quart batches to insure the proper blending of flavors. The dressing will stay fresh for quite a while in the refrigerator.

SALAD

Spinach for 4
Fresh mushrooms, sliced
Bacon bits, freshly chopped
Burgundy Dressing (see below)

1. Clean spinach and drain well. Break into pieces and chill.
2. Toss with dressing and garnish with mushrooms and bacon bits.

BURGUNDY DRESSING

1 cup red wine vinegar
2 cups salad oil
2 teaspoons sugar
1 teaspoon salt
2 teaspoons crushed garlic
3/4 cup red Burgundy wine (such as Mondavi)
1 teaspoon crushed oregano leaves
1 teaspoon crushed basil leaves
1/2 teaspoon white pepper
2 teaspoons Worcestershire sauce
1/2 cup fresh lemon juice

1. Combine all ingredients and chill. Makes 1 quart.

STEAK WITH ARTICHOKES AND SOUR CREAM

Be sure filets are cut from a beef tender. About five to seven pounds is the best weight for the tender. The sauce with sour cream is unusual with beef.

4 tablespoons butter
8 (1-inch thick) filets (2 per person)
4 teaspoons chopped fresh parsley
4 tablespoons chopped fresh chives
4 artichoke hearts, sliced
1½ ounces brandy
1 cup dry white wine (such as Chablis)
3/4 cup brown sauce
1 cup sour cream

1. Melt the butter in a flambé pan over medium heat.
2. Sauté the filets, and cook to order.
3. Add the parsley, chives and artichoke hearts.
4. Flambé with brandy.
5. Remove the steak to a hot plate.
6. Add wine to the pan and bring it to a boil, scraping up pan juices. Reduce heat, add the brown sauce and sour cream, and stir to blend well. Cook for 1 minute and serve the sauce over the steak. *Do not let sour cream boil.*

COURTLANDTS

BROCCOLI WITH LEMON BUTTER

1 large bunch fresh broccoli
1 cup water
Salt and pepper
1 cup melted butter
Juice of 1 lemon

1. Clean the broccoli and break it into branches. Bring the water to a boil and add salt and pepper.
2. Cook the broccoli with the seasoned water in covered pan until crisp-tender.
3. Drain and arrange the broccoli on a platter.
4. Serve with melted butter to which you have added the lemon juice.

COURTLANDT'S

CRÊPES ROMANOFF

4 tablespoons butter
1 cup sugar
Juice of 2 lemons
Juice of 2 oranges
2 tablespoons grated orange rind
1 ounce Grand Marnier liqueur
1/2 ounce Cointreau liqueur
8 pre-made crêpes
32 large strawberries
3/4 ounce 151-proof rum

1. Melt the butter in flambé pan over medium heat.
2. Add the sugar, lemon and orange juice, orange rind, Grand Marnier and Cointreau. Cook until sauce thickens.
3. Add the crêpes to the sauce, one at a time, turning each in order to coat both sides.
4. Fold 4 large strawberries into each crêpe and arrange all crêpes in a pan.
5. Flambé with rum and serve *at once* on hot plates.

Houstonians love crêpe desserts. We believe that crêpes should be fresh—*never frozen*. Use a crêpe pan rather than a crêpe machine.

D'Amico's Italian Restaurant

Dinner for Four

Caponatina

Minestra di Lenticchie
(Lentil Soup)

Vermicelli alla Granchia con Carciofi Marinara
(Vermicelli with Crab and Artichokes)

Bracioluna

Frittata di Pomodori Verdi
(Green Tomato Frittata)

Cannoli

Espresso

Wine:

With Soup and Vermicelli — Corvo Salaparuta (white)

With Bracioluna — Brunello di Montalcino

Nash D'Amico, Damian Mandola,
Charles Petronella, Owners

Osvaldo Vasquez, Chef

Cousins Damian Mandola, Nash D'Amico, and Charles Petronella opened D'Amico's because they believe that people would enjoy their homestyle Italian food. All are from large Italian families who lived in Houston for years.

The idea for their first restaurant came while they were in college. "We always found that our cooking was a little different from what we could buy in an Italian restaurant." In 1975 they opened Damian's Fine Italian Foods, in Huntsville. "We thought we were going to have a sandwich and pizza place, but the people in Huntsville turned us into a full-fledged restaurant.

"We always wanted to open a restaurant in Houston," says Mandola. "That was our dream. We researched the area for over a year before we found the right spot." Mandola concentrates on the restaurant's kitchen, D'Amico handles the administration, and Petronella manages the Huntsville restaurant.

Rose colored walls set the decor. Green plants, pale pink linens, hanging parasol lamps, and framed family portraits provide a pleasantly elegant setting.

"We have found that people in Houston are looking for something different. They are more knowledgeable, more traveled. They've been to Italy and know Italian food is not just pasta. A lot of restaurants lack friendliness and become very cold when they become elegant and have good service. We hope to achieve good service, but keep that touch of personal friendliness and pleasant atmosphere, because Italians are amiable people and like to have a good time."

2407 Westheimer

CAPONATINA

When guests arrive, set out a relish tray consisting of Caponatina, Genoa salami, caciocavallo and provolone cheeses and bread sticks. It should be just enough to whet the appetite. Accompany with an aperitif, such as chilled dry vermouth, or Campari and soda. This recipe makes about two quarts, but you can store it in the refrigerator in tightly closed, sterilized jars. It may be made as much as six weeks ahead of time, and refrigerated until ready to serve.

1/2 cup olive oil
1 large onion, chopped
1 cup chopped celery
2 pounds unpeeled eggplant, cut in 1-inch cubes
3½ ounces tomato paste
1 cup water
1 pound green Sicilian olives, pitted
1 (2-ounce) jar unsalted capers, drained
Salt and pepper to taste
1 heaping teaspoon sugar
1/4 cup red wine vinegar

1. Heat olive oil in a large skillet. Add onion and celery and cook until almost tender. Remove and place in a bowl.
2. In the same skillet, sauté eggplant until light brown. Remove and set aside.
3. In the same pan, combine tomato paste and water. Cook over medium heat, stirring until completely blended.
4. Add olives, eggplant, capers, onion, celery and salt and pepper to taste. Mix well.
5. Bring to a boil over high heat. Lower heat and simmer for 5 minutes.
6. Add sugar and vinegar. Stir and simmer for 1/2 minute.
7. Remove from heat and cool.

D'AMICO'S

MINESTRA DI LENTICCHIE
(Lentil Soup)

1 cup lentils
1 rib celery, chopped
1 small onion, chopped
1 clove garlic, minced
Small piece of prosciutto rind, slab bacon or salt pork
Pinch of oregano
1 mashed canned plum tomato
1¾ quarts water
1/4 cup olive oil

1. Place all ingredients except olive oil in a stock pot and bring the mixture to a boil.
2. Cover and lower heat. Simmer for 30 minutes.
3. Remove lid and simmer for an additional 20 minutes, or until the lentils are tender. Season with salt and pepper.
4. Add olive oil, stir well, and serve.

Italian cooking is not covered up with sauces, and it's not rich in cream like French cooking, so you can't hide the natural taste. It's got to be there. If the food's fresh, you're more than half way there.

VERMICELLI ALLA GRANCHIA CON CARCIOFI MARINARA

(Vermicelli with Crab and Artichokes)

1 pound vermicelli
1 (2 pound 3-ounce) can plum tomatoes
1/4 cup olive oil
1 large or 2 medium cloves garlic, finely chopped
2 anchovy filets
1/2 teaspoon oregano
Salt and freshly ground black pepper
Pinch of crushed red pepper (optional)
1 pound cooked crabmeat with juices
4 or 5 artichoke hearts, sliced

1. Use a fork to mash tomatoes to a fine consistency. Set aside.
2. Heat olive oil in a large saucepan and sauté garlic over low heat for 3 to 4 minutes.
3. Add the anchovies and sauté for 1 minute more.
4. Add tomatoes, oregano, salt and pepper. Simmer 30 to 45 minutes, stirring occasionally.
5. About 5 minutes before serving, add crabmeat, juices and artichoke hearts.
6. Boil vermicelli in 6 quarts salted water until *al dente*—just firm to the tooth. Drain and arrange on a deep platter.
7. Toss with half of the sauce. Pour the rest of sauce into a sauce boat and serve with vermicelli.

BRACIOLUNA

(Stuffed Beef Roll)

***This style of braciole is typical of Sicily. It is rolled up jelly roll fashion. The mixture is dry, but becomes moist after cooking. An alternative to this recipe is to place the Bracioluna, after browning, in your favorite tomato sauce for the last hour of cooking, then remove and slice.

It is also possible to cook the meat and make a sauce in advance that can be placed on the table at serving time.***

8 sprigs parsley, chopped
1 clove garlic, minced
1/2 cup fresh bread crumbs (preferably made from French bread)
3 tablespoons freshly grated Romano cheese
2 tablespoons chopped bell pepper
Salt and pepper to taste
1½ pounds round steak, boned, cut 1/4-inch thick
2 tablespoons olive oil
2 hard cooked eggs, sliced
1/4 cup oil for browning

1. Combine parsley, garlic, bread crumbs, cheese, bell pepper, salt and pepper. Mix well and add a little water to make a paste.
2. Pound the round steak a little on both sides. Lay it out flat on a counter or table.
3. Brush olive oil over the steak.
4. Spread bread crumb mixture over the steak and then lay hard cooked egg slices on top. Fold in the sides of the steak and roll up just as you would a jelly roll. Tie securely with string.
5. Heat 1/4 cup oil in a sauté pan and brown steak on all sides. Remove and place in a roasting pan with oil and drippings.
6. Add 3/4 cup water. Cover pan and roast the meat at 350 degrees for 45 minutes. When done, remove string and cut in 1-inch slices.
7. Place slices on serving tray with pan juices and serve.

MOGU

***This is a Sicilian pesto. The recipe comes from Damian Mandola's mother and grandmother and is strictly for garlic lovers! It can also be used on other roasted, broiled or charbroiled meats or poultry.

The sauce can be made well in advance and stored indefinitely at room temperature. Stir well before using.***

10 cloves garlic, chopped
1/2 teaspoon oregano
10 mint leaves, chopped, or 1 teaspoon dried mint
4 basil leaves, chopped, or 1/2 teaspoon dried basil
1/2 pint olive oil
1/4 pint white vinegar
2 teaspoons lemon juice
Salt and pepper to taste

1. Place all ingredients in a mortar and pulverize with a pestle.
2. Put mashed ingredients in a pint jar.
3. Add liquid ingredients and shake well. Stir well before using.

NOTE: Mogu can be made in a blender or food processor but *be sure to add a little oil, first*.

FRITTATA DI POMODORI VERDI
(Green Tomato Frittata)

Almost any fresh vegetable in season can be substituted for the green tomatoes in this dish. Zucchini, yellow squash or a mixture of mushrooms and artichoke hearts are all good.

4 large green tomatoes
1 cup plus 1 tablespoon olive oil
1 cup all-purpose flour
6 eggs
Salt and freshly ground pepper

1. Wash the tomatoes well and cut them into 1/2-inch slices.
2. Heat 1 cup oil in a frying pan. Do *not* use more than 1 cup, as tomato slices should not be completely covered. While oil is heating, flour tomatoes.
3. When oil begins to sizzle, place only as many tomato slices in pan as will make a single layer. Sauté until golden brown on both sides, then drain on paper towel. Sprinkle with salt and pepper. Fry the remaining tomatoes in the same manner.
4. Beat the eggs very lightly with a pinch of salt. Set aside.
5. Heat 1 tablespoon olive oil in an omelet pan. When hot, add the tomato slices to the pan. (The slices will be reduced in size from having been sautéed, so they should all fit in one layer.)
6. Pour the eggs over the tomato slices. When the eggs are well set and the frittata is well detached from the bottom of the pan, place a plate, face down, over the pan. Holding the plate firmly, reverse the pan and turn the frittata out onto it.
7. Return the pan to the heat. Carefully slide the frittata into the pan to cook the other side.
8. After 1 minute, reverse the frittata onto a serving dish. It may be served hot or cold.

CANNOLI

Cannoli is a true Sicilian tradition. The casing is made of a wine dough and the filling is a delicious ricotta cheese mixture. To make cannoli it is necessary to have some metal tubes about 1/2 inch in diameter and about 5 inches long. You may be able to get a hardware store to cut aluminum tubing to length for you.

SHELLS

2 cups all-purpose flour
1/2 teaspoon cinnamon
1 tablespoon sugar
Pinch of salt
1 heaping tablespoon lard
1 egg
1 cup sweet Italian red wine such as Lambrusco or Marsala

1. Sift flour, cinnamon, sugar and salt into a bowl. Cut in the lard and rub it well into the flour.
2. Add the egg and knead it into the flour.
3. Gradually add enough wine to make a firm dough. The amount will vary slightly according to the type of flour used.
4. Knead the dough until smooth and elastic.
5. Place a bowl over the dough and let it stand, covered, for about 20 minutes. *This will make rolling easier.*

6. Cut off one-fourth of the dough and roll it out paper thin. Cut the thin sheet of pastry dough into 3-inch squares.
7. Repeat until all the dough is rolled out and cut in squares.
8. Place a metal tube diagonally on each square and bring the two corners over to meet in the middle. Press to seal.
9. In a deep pan, heat enough vegetable oil for deep frying. Oil should be very hot, about 375 to 400 degrees. Tubes should be completely immersed in oil and shells should come out looking blistered.
10. Cook shells, two at a time, until golden brown. Remove with a slotted spoon and drain on paper towel.
11. As soon as the pastry is cool, gently remove the tubes.

NOTE: This recipe makes about two dozen shells, more than needed for four persons. The extra shells may be prepared, then stored in an airtight container for later use.

FILLING

1/2 pound ricotta cheese
1/2 cup powdered sugar
1/2 cup honey
1 tablespoon whipped cream
1/2 cup pecan pieces
1/4 cup semisweet chocolate chips
1/3 cup diced citron or candied pineapple
5 glace cherries, chopped
1 tablespoon chocolate extract
Decorations: Green sugar crystals, pecan pieces, powdered sugar

1. Combine ricotta, powdered sugar, honey and whipped cream in a bowl and blend well with electric mixer until creamy.
2. Fold in the pecans, chocolate chips, citron and cherries.
3. Remove about 6 tablespoons of the filling and place in another small bowl. Add chocolate extract and mix well. Refrigerate both vanilla and chocolate fillings until ready to use.
4. Just before serving, fill shells with vanilla filling and spread chocolate on the outside.
5. Sprinkle green sugar crystals on each end of the cannoli, then dip each end in pecan pieces.
6. Arrange cannoli on a dish and sprinkle with powdered sugar. Serve immediately.

Foulard's Restaurant

Dinner for Four

Oysters Ruth

Chilled Cream, Foulard

Poached Filet of Sole, Duglere

Lemon Sorbet

Roast Rack of Lamb Persille

Potato Croquette, Sautéed Belgian Endive, Baked Tomato

Chocolate Soufflé with Cream Anglaise

Coffee

Wine:

With Oysters — Château Carbonnieux, 1972

With Lamb — Château Monbousquet, 1973

With Soufflé — Piesporter Goldtröpfchen Spätlese, 1975

Edmond M. Foulard, Chef-Owner

George Finch, Chef

This elegant restaurant with a water wheel, rough stone, and heavy beam exterior is the culmination of a dream for chef-owner Edmond M. Foulard. Canadian born of French parentage, it was always Foulard's ambition to come to America. He apprenticed in Nantes and later acquired his own restaurants in Paris. He came to this country after World War II, moving to Houston in 1962. He and his wife, Annemarie, loved Houston and decided to open their own restaurant in 1966 at the River Oaks apartment. Foulard moved to another location in 1971 and then to the present restaurant, which he personally designed, in 1976.

He has resumed his demonstration cooking school, which began at River Oaks and has been awarded membership in several chefs' organizations, among them, the American Academy of Chefs. Foulard holds the Golden Toque award from the American Institute of Chefs and is a member of the Chevalier de la Confrerie de la Chaine des Rotisseurs. His restaurant has received the Holiday Award for 1977 and 1978.

Soft greens, wainscoting, gold wall sconces, antiques, and high-backed chairs in the dining room complement a mural done by Houston artist Nione Carlson.

Foulard stresses fine ingredients and cooking methods rather than fancy equipment. Many feel that as a chef he has no peer. "I feel that we appeal to the cosmopolite. We appeal to people who have traveled and who know food. The restaurant is all my life."

10001 Westheimer

OYSTERS RUTH

20 to 24 oysters (5 or 6 per person)
Flour
Eggwash (2 eggs, 1/4 cup milk or half-and-half, salt and pepper)
Fresh white bread crumbs
Grated lemon rind
Crushed blanched almonds
Mustard Sauce (see below)

1. Detach oysters from their shells. Rinse them in cold water and pat dry.
2. Dredge in flour.
3. Dip in egg wash, then in bread crumbs into which you have mixed a grated lemon rind and a few crushed almonds.
4. Deep fry at about 325 to 350 degrees until golden blond. Drain well. Sprinkle with a little salt and serve with Mustard Sauce.

MUSTARD SAUCE

1 small shallot, finely chopped
1/2 cup dry white wine
1 cup whipping cream
1 tablespoon dry mustard

1. Sauté the shallot in butter. Add wine and allow it to reduce until almost dry.
2. Pour in the whipping cream. Bring to a boil.
3. Mix in mustard (1 tablespoon or to taste). Whip until smooth. Strain and serve hot.

FOULARD'S

CHILLED CREAM, FOULARD

3 to 4 white leeks
Butter
1/2 cup dried green split peas
1 quart light chicken stock
Salt and pepper
Freshly grated nutmeg
Whipping cream

1. Wash leeks and slice or dice them. Make them "sweat" a little by placing them in a pot with a piece of fresh butter, covering the pot and placing it on the corner of the stove.
2. Add the peas and cover with chicken stock. Simmer until the peas are tender.
3. Season to taste with salt, pepper and nutmeg. Let cool and mix in a blender until smooth.
4. Finish by adding enough whipping cream to make 1 quart. Serve *very* chilled.

A recipe is only a guide. I always tell my students that they must not be afraid if they go too far, or too short. It doesn't matter as long as the result is good. If it isn't the same recipe, they have created a new one!

POACHED FILET OF SOLE, DUGLERE

4 filets of sole
Court Bouillon (see below)
2 finely chopped shallots
1 tomato, peeled and seeded
Freshly chopped parsley
1/2 cup rather thick, fish velouté sauce (cream sauce made with fish stock instead of milk)
1/2 cup Hollandaise sauce
1/2 cup whipped cream

1. Detach filets of sole from the bones. Poach in Court Bouillon. Keep enough stock above the filets to keep them hot and to prevent them from drying out. Use the rest of the stock to prepare the sauce.
2. To the stock, add the shallots and tomato which has been cut into small pieces. Bring to a fast boil and let the liquid reduce. Add fresh chopped parsley at the last minute.
3. Add fish velouté, Hollandaise and whipped cream.
4. Season to taste.
5. Arrange sole filets on a serving platter. Wipe them dry and cover with the sauce. Glaze under a salamander or broiler.

COURT BOUILLON

1/2 carrot
1 small onion
1/2 celery rib
3 or 4 parsley stems
3 or 4 peppercorns
1 small bay leaf
Salt
Water or dry white wine such as Chablis or Rhine
Fish bones

1. Finely slice the carrot, onion, celery and parsley.
2. Mix them with white peppercorns, bay leaf and a little salt and add to water or water and dry white wine in equal proportions. Add fish bones if desired.
3. Strain and cool before using.

FOULARD'S

LEMON SORBET

This is served as a palate refresher between the fish course and the entrée. It can be finished with either heavy cream or whipped cream.

1 cup sauterne
Juice of 1 lemon and 1/2 orange
Grated lemon rind
1 cup water
3/4 cup sugar
1/2 cup heavy cream or whipped cream

1. Mix sauterne, lemon and orange juices, lemon rind, water and sugar and bring to a boil. Simmer for *exactly* 5 minutes.
2. Let mixture cool, then freeze.
3. Break up with a wire whip and finish by adding heavy cream and whipping until smooth, or by folding already-beaten cream into the mixture.
4. Freeze well before serving.

To me, food is sacred. It is to be handled with respect. There is no real secret to cooking at home. The best thing is to make things simpler.

FOULARD'S

ROAST RACK OF LAMB PERSILLE

For bread crumbs, we use regular white sandwich bread. Trim the crusts, then press them through a colander with large holes, like a frying basket. To the brown sauce, we usually add the browned bones. After they have been browned in the oven, drain off the fat and add the bones to a regular brown sauce. Strain before serving.

Double rack of lamb, trimmed as if you were to cut lamb chops
Salt and pepper
2 cups fresh white bread crumbs
1 egg yolk
1 tablespoon finely chopped shallots
1 chopped garlic clove
2 tablespoons freshly chopped parsley
1/4 cup melted butter
Brown Sauce

1. Rub the lamb with salt and pepper and roast it in a hot (475-degree) oven for about 10 minutes. (Cover the ribs with foil.)
2. Allow the lamb to cool slightly and then coat it with a mixture of the bread crumbs, egg yolk, shallots and garlic (which have been sautéed in butter). Finish with parsley and melted butter and return the lamb to the oven.
3. Reduce heat to about 400 degrees and roast again until the crust is firm and the meat is done to desired state. If it browns too rapidly, cover with foil.
4. Serve with a brown sauce to which you may add a teaspoon of freshly chopped mint leaves.

FOULARD'S

POTATO CROQUETTES

2 potatoes, peeled and boiled
Salt, pepper and nutmeg to taste
2 eggs, beaten
Whipping cream
1 or 2 slices crushed crisp bacon
1 tablespoon chopped onion, sauteed in a little butter
1 teaspoon chopped chives or parsley
1 slice grated cheddar cheese
Egg wash
Fresh white bread crumbs
Oil

1. Drain potatoes well and dry them a little in a low oven, or bake them and scoop out the pulp.
2. Mash the potatoes and season with salt, pepper and nutmeg. Add beaten eggs and just enough whipping cream to hold the mixture together and yet keep it very dry.
3. If desired, add bacon, onion, chives and grated cheese. Let cool.
4. Form into croquette shapes or balls.
5. Dust with flour, dip in egg wash, then in bread crumbs.
6. Deep fry (or pan fry if you shape them flat) just enough to color them and sear the exterior.
7. Finish heating the croquettes in a hot oven.

BAKED TOMATO

2 tomatoes, well-ripened
Salt and pepper
Melted butter

1. Cut the tomatoes in half. Season with salt and pepper.
2. Sprinkle with melted butter and bake in the oven.

With good ingredients, even if you don't have the best equipment, you can still make beautiful things.

SAUTÉED BELGIAN ENDIVE

Endive for 4
Salted water
Flour
Clarified butter
Butter

1. Trim and blanch whole endive for a few minutes in boiling salted water. Drain and dry well.
2. Dredge in flour.
3. Sauté the endive in clarified butter on all sides until golden blond. If still a little too firm, finish cooking in the oven after discarding the frying butter.
4. When done, add a fresh piece of butter, let the butter melt, and serve.

I cook any kind of dish; not necessarily just French food. But I cook with the French principles and add my own style, what I could call, if it were not already done a little too often, "new French cooking". I add no fat or grease. When I sauté a fish or chicken, I sauté it in clarified butter. As soon as it is colored, not cooked, but just colored, I discard the clarified butter and place the food, dry, in the oven. Then I finish it with melted butter, but not fat. I do not serve fried fat or fried butter.

FOULARD'S

CHOCOLATE SOUFFLÉ WITH CREAM ANGLAISE

It is very important to keep the flour-sugar-butter paste dry and hot. Work in eggs very well and beat quickly and thoroughly before adding each additional egg.

3 ounces flour (3/4 cup)
3 ounces sugar (6 tablespoons)
3 ounces butter (6 tablespoons)
1½ cups milk or half-and-half, heated just to boiling point
1½ tablespoons pure vanilla extract
1½ ounces semisweet chocolate
6 egg yolks
9 egg whites
6 tablespoons sugar

1. Knead the flour, 3 ounces sugar and butter into a paste with a spatula. Add it to the boiling milk, into which you have already put the vanilla and the chocolate and let chocolate melt. *Do this carefully*; if the liquid is too hot the chocolate will become grainy. Preheat oven to 325 degrees.
2. Cook for about 2 minutes, stirring constantly, until the paste that is forming detaches itself from the pan and spatula.
3. Add the egg yolks, one at a time, mixing well until all the egg yolks are absorbed. Keep warm.
4. Meanwhile, whip the egg whites very firm with a pinch of salt, gradually adding the 6 tablespoons sugar.
5. Fold egg whites gently into the warm chocolate paste with a spatula.
6. Butter a 2½-quart soufflé mold, then coat it with sugar.
7. Fill soufflé dish to about four-fifths of its height.
8. Bake at 325 degrees for 40 to 45 minutes. Serve immediately with Cream Anglaise.

FOULARD'S

CREAM ANGLAISE

4 egg yolks
2½ ounces sugar
1 cup milk or half-and-half, heated to boiling
1/4 vanilla stick or other desired flavoring to taste

1. Beat egg yolks and sugar until the mixture is smooth and forms ribbons when the beater is lifted. Meanwhile, heat milk.
2. Pour a little hot milk over the egg yolks, stir quickly to blend. Return to the milk in the pan, stirring constantly.
3. Continue to stir constantly until the mixture coats a wooden spoon. Do not let the mixture boil.
4. Strain and stir until cool to the touch.

Being a chef is not enough. You have to work at it all your life. You have to learn all your life because there is always something new. If you are really interested and study all the time, then you make and create new recipes. *Then* you are a chef. Otherwise, you are just another worker.

Gaspair's

Dinner for Six

Fried Provolone Cheese in Red Italian Sauce

Shrimp Bisque

Cucumber Salad

Trout Gaspair

Flan

Gaspair's Continental Coffee

Wine:

*Bâtard-Montrachet, 1975 or
Sonoma Chardonnay, 1975*

Gasper De George, Owner

Myriam Font, Chef

GASPAIR'S

Gaspair's is owner Gasper De George's first restaurant. "I grew up in the hotel and restaurant business because it was my father's and grandfather's work. My grandfather built several hotels here, including some of the finest of early Houston.

"Our location is a natural one; there have been restaurants here for thirty years. I think that this contributes to our success. Also, this is a small restaurant and we give it a lot of personal attention.

De George wanted an animal logo and finally decided on the giraffe. Giraffes are featured on the menus and matchcovers as well as in paintings and accessories. The entry wall is hung with framed cartoons and snapshots of regular customers and celebrities. De George's daughter, Sharon Ruse, shares business responsibilities. Another daughter, Cynthia MacCurdy, decorated the restaurant.

The restaurant dining room resembles a gazebo with its white latticework and emerald green carpeting. Rotating art shows offer paintings for sale.

Gaspair's is known for several unique dishes, special gourmet dinners and after-dinner drinks.

3941 San Felipe

GASPAIR'S

FRIED PROVOLONE WITH RED ITALIAN SAUCE

6 (6-ounce) provolone cheese slices about 1/2-inch thick each
3 eggs
2 cups milk
Dash of salt and pepper
1 tablespoon fresh chopped parsley
3 cups bread crumbs
3 cups flour
Tomato Sauce (see recipe below)

1. Mix eggs, milk, salt, pepper and parsley and beat well. Place the bread crumbs and flour in separate bowls.
2. Dip a cheese slice in the egg mixture, then flour, then egg, then flour again.
3. Dip the cheese in the egg mixture a third time, then in bread crumbs.
4. Deep fat fry at 350 degrees until golden brown.
5. Serve with Red Italian Sauce.

RED ITALIAN SAUCE

2 small onions, finely chopped
1/2 bell pepper, finely chopped
1 clove garlic, finely chopped
1/4 cup butter
1 teaspoon oregano
1/4 cup Burgundy wine
3 tablespoons tomato paste
1 (16-ounce) can whole peeled tomatoes
3/4 cup water—or more if needed
Dash of salt and pepper

1. Sauté onions, pepper, and garlic in butter until done.
2. Combine all ingredients with the onion mixture and simmer for 45 minutes.
3. Serve the tomato sauce on a plate and top with fried provolone. Sprinkle with fresh chopped parsley.

This recipe was brought to us by a former manager who was Argentine. The appetizer is very popular in Argentina and it reflects the Italian influence on that cuisine. Remember to have the cheese cold for proper melting.

GASPAIR'S

SHRIMP BISQUE

2 large onions, finely chopped
1 cup butter
Flour
1½ pounds shrimp
8 cups water
2 bay leaves
Salt and pepper

1. In a 5-quart pot, sauté the onions in butter until soft. Add enough flour to absorb butter.
2. Combine the shrimp, water, bay leaves and salt and pepper and bring water to a boil. Continue boiling for 6 minutes.
3. Pour the stock from the shrimp into the onion-flour mixture. Simmer for 45 minutes to 1 hour, or until thickened, stirring occasionally.
4. Chop the shrimp into small pieces and add to the mixture. Cook 15 minutes longer and serve.

Originated by chef Myriam Font, this bisque recipe uses whole shrimp (heads and all) for the stock instead of heavy cream. The result is fewer calories and a good shrimp flavor. After the stock is made, the shrimp is removed, cleaned and chopped.

CUCUMBER SALAD

2 cucumbers
1 cup sour cream
Juice of 1 lemon
3 tablespoons olive oil
3 tablespoons chopped fresh parsley
Dash of salt and pepper

1. Partially peel cucumbers. Thinly slice.
2. Combine remaining ingredients and mix well.
3. Mix with cucumber slices. Chill and serve.

Our cucumber salad comes from Lebanon where it is called 'Desert Salad'.

GASPAIR'S

TROUT GASPAIR

6 (8-ounce) filets of fresh trout
1½ cups butter
1/2 cup white wine
Juice of 2 lemons

1. Combine the melted butter, wine and lemon juice.
2. Bake the trout in this mixture for about 15 to 20 minutes at 375 degrees.
3. Serve with Gaspair Sauce.

GASPAIR SAUCE

1/2 pound fresh mushrooms, sliced
1 cup butter
1 (14-ounce) can artichoke hearts, sliced
2 tablespoons capers
Juice of 2 lemons
1/2 cup white wine
Dash of granulated garlic
Salt and pepper to taste
Freshly chopped parsley

1. Sauté mushrooms in butter until soft.
2. Add artichoke hearts and capers and cook for 3 minutes.
3. Add remaining ingredients and cook for 5 minutes.
4. Place each filet on a plate and top with sauce. Sprinkle with freshly chopped parsley.

This is a creation of owner Gasper De George. Use Chablis for best results.

FLAN

2 cups, 5 ounces sugar
7 eggs
2 tablespoons vanilla extract
1 tablespoon rum extract
1 quart milk

1. Pour 9 ounces sugar, eggs, vanilla and rum into a mixer bowl and whip with an electric mixer for 3 minutes.
2. Bring milk to a boil (scald), cool slightly, and add it to the egg mixture.
3. Pour 1½ cups sugar into a heavy stainless steel pan and cook carefully over low heat, stirring constantly, until it melts and turns a light brown color. Cover bottom and side of pan and let it cool for 10 minutes.
4. Add milk-egg mixture.
5. Place the pan in a larger pan filled with 3 inches of water and bake at 375 degrees for 1 hour or until light brown.

One of Myriam Font's South American recipes.

GASPAIR'S CONTINENTAL COFFEE

Per person:
1½ ounces coconut rum
1/2 ounce Kahlúa
Freshly brewed coffee
Whipped cream

1. Pour rum and Kahlúa into a crystal mug.
2. Fill with hot coffee.
3. Garnish with whipped cream.

The Great Caruso

Dinner for Six

French-Fried Zucchini with Béarnaise Sauce

Shrimp in Ale Batter

Fish or Shrimp with Sauce au Beurre Antoinette

Royal English Trifle

Kahlua Freeze

Wine:

With Zucchini and Shrimp — Château de Costis Entre-Deux-Mers

Toni, Spero and Ernie Criezis, Owners

Walter Carter, Executive Chef

Francois Verdier, Chef

The Great Caruso is a total experience, not just a restaurant. Its concept goes back to the supper club tradition when diners were royally entertained and ate amid posh surroundings. It was created and built by the Criezis family as a showplace for singers and old-fashioned stage entertainment combined with fine dining. Since its opening in September, 1977, it has drawn almost standing-room-only crowds every evening and there usually is a two-week backup for weekend reservations.

Toni Renee and husband Ernie Criezis have brought Houston major-name entertainment since 1966. The Great Caruso is the latest of their unique restaurants which range from modified New York delis to after-theater spots. All are decorated and furnished with one-of-a-kind antiques and accessories found on their worldwide travels.

"We never take a vacation. Vacations are always treasure hunts," says Toni Renee. Many of the antiques for The Great Caruso came from Europe or old demolished opera houses. An extensive collection of opera memorabilia decorates the walls. A twelve-ton marble pulpit and marble staircase, built in Italy a century ago, serves as one of four singing stages. These antiques plus stained glass, opulent chandeliers, palms, and art work are a feast for the eye.

The spectacular 300-seat restaurant places diners in tiered rows around a stage area. The walls reverberate to the music of professional opera singers and waiters. You may hear operatic arias, Irish songs, Broadway music or see dancing vignettes such as 1940's-style tap dance routines. Toni Renee, a professional singer, performs weekends.

The Great Caruso is inspiring among Houstonians the new habit of late dining. The limited after-hours menu is popular, too, and there is a separate menu for after-dinner sweets and drinks where a variety of liqueur freezes, ice creams and fresh daiquiris are offered.

Briar Park Drive at Westheimer
in Carillon West Center

THE GREAT CARUSO

FRENCH FRIED ZUCCHINI WITH BÉARNAISE SAUCE

This dish delighted British singing star Shirley Bassey when she visited The Great Caruso just after its opening in late 1977.

3 zucchini
Flour
Milk
Cracker meal
Hot oil
Béarnaise Sauce

1. Wash zucchini; dry and slice in long, vertical strips.
2. Dip in flour, then in milk.
3. Roll slices in cracker meal.
4. Fry until golden brown in hot oil. Serve with Béarnaise, either on top or alongside the zucchini. Hollandaise may be substituted for the Béarnaise Sauce.

BÉARNAISE SAUCE

5 white peppercorns, crushed
2 sprigs parsley
1/2 to 1 tablespoon chopped onion or shallots
2 tablespoons wine or tarragon vinegar
4 tablespoons water
3 egg yolks
6 to 8 ounces butter, melted
1 tablespoon chopped fresh parsley, chervil and tarragon, fresh, dried or pickled
Salt to taste

1. Mix the peppercorns, parsley, onion, vinegar and water. Boil until the mixture has reduced to about one-third of its original volume. Strain and return to the saucepan.
2. Beat in the egg yolks. Simmer the sauce in a double boiler over, not in, boiling water until it begins to thicken.
3. Add the melted butter carefully, whisking constantly until the sauce is thick, bright and foamy.
4. Add the chopped herbs and taste for seasoning. Bernaise Sauce should be served *immediately*. If it has to be kept hot, place the uncovered pan into a hot water bath.

THE GREAT CARUSO

SHRIMP IN ALE BATTER
(Southern Fried Shrimp à la Caruso)

***After eating this dish, the Prince of Malaysia, a guest at the Great Caruso one evening, demanded to join the entertainers on stage and sang a credible rendition of "Cotton Fields Back Home".

Dark beer or Guinness ale is particularly good in the ale batter, although any beer or ale may be used. Be sure that the shrimp are well-coated with flour. You must use either self-rising flour or 3 cups all-purpose flour plus 3 teaspoons baking powder and 1½ teaspoons salt. Draining the shrimp on cheesecloth until they are ready to serve keeps them crisp, but allows the oil to drain.***

30 shrimp, cleaned, deveined, with tails intact
Fresh lemon juice
Salt and pepper
Worcestershire sauce
Tabasco sauce
2 cups whole milk
2 cups ale or beer
4 eggs
Salt and pepper to taste
3 cups self-rising flour
2 tablespoons paprika
Oil for deep frying

1. Marinate the shrimp in lemon juice seasoned to taste with salt and pepper, Worcestershire sauce and Tabasco sauce.
2. Combine milk, ale, eggs, salt and pepper and mix thoroughly.
3. Combine the flour and paprika. Roll the shrimp in the mixture; it should be well coated.
4. Add the remaining flour mixture to the egg batter and dip the shrimp in the new mixture.
5. Deep-fry at 350 degrees until golden brown. Serve with your favorite remoulade or red sauce.

THE GREAT CARUSO

FISH OR SHRIMP WITH SAUCE AU BEURRE ANTOINETTE

Texas' own popular Senator Jack Ogg specially requests any dish that comes prepared with this fine sauce. It is absolutely delicious served over fish, boiled shrimp, lobster, steamed clams or mussels. It's good with beef, too. If you do serve beef, I'd suggest Château de Lescours St. Émilion as an accompanying wine.

Fish filets for 6, or 36 large shrimp (10–15 count per pound)
Sauce au Beurre Antoinette (see below)

1. Poach or broil fish filets, or boil shrimp.
2. Prepare sauce and serve.

SAUCE AU BEURRE ANTOINETTE

1/2 pound butter
1 cup fresh fish stock or chicken broth
1/4 teaspoon paprika
1/4 teaspoon thyme
1 teaspoon chopped fresh chives
1 teaspoon chopped fresh tarragon
2 teaspoons chopped fresh parsley
Salt and pepper to taste
1/4 teaspoon Worcestershire sauce
Tabasco sauce to taste
2 tablespoons, or more, fresh lemon juice
3 tablespoons cornstarch
2 tablespoons water

1. In a saucepan, melt the butter and add stock and all the seasonings, including the lemon juice.
2. Bring the liquid to a boil and simmer briefly.
3. Combine the cornstarch with water and gradually stir it into the mixture.
4. Simmer, stirring, until thickened and smooth.

THE GREAT CARUSO

ROYAL ENGLISH TRIFLE

This is Toni's own special English Trifle. It was recommended by the Lord Provost, the Honorable Mayor of the City of Glasgow, David Hodge, on his visit to Houston at the opening of British Caledonian Airlines service here. This recipe is enough to generously serve twelve.

5 rectangular slices pound cake, 1-inch thick, cubed
2 ounces sherry
2 ounces Amaretto liqueur
2 cups fresh or canned fruit salad with juice
1 (3-ounce) package cherry gelatin
1 (3 5/8-ounce) package vanilla flavor instant pudding
Freshly whipped cream
Chocolate sprinkles

1. Place cubed cake in the bottom of a glass bowl and soak it with sherry and Amaretto.
2. Top with fruit and juice.
3. Prepare gelatin according to package directions and chill until slightly thickened.
4. Prepare pudding according to package directions and pour over the fruit. Prepare and pour the gelatin over the pudding.
5. Refrigerate until properly set. *It's best to let this stand overnight.*
6. Garnish with freshly whipped cream and chocolate sprinkles.

KAHLÚA FREEZE

If you can't find vanilla bean ice cream, add a little vanilla flavoring.

Per person:

6 small scoops vanilla bean ice cream (such as Barricini)
2 ounces Kahlúa
Whipped cream
Cocoa powder (such as Droste's)

1. Mix ice cream and Kahlúa in a blender, until thick and smooth.
2. Garnish with whipped cream and sprinkle with a dusting of cocoa.
Serve in stemmed tulip glasses.

HARRIGAN'S

Dinner for Six

Oysters Capri

Cajun Gumbo

Fettuccine all' "Alfredo"

Snapper Riviera

Crêpes Marnier

Irish Coffee

Wine:
With Oysters and Gumbo — Gewürztraminer
With Fettuccine and Snapper — Bâtard-Montrachet

Jim Harrigan, Owner
Joe Lennon
Jacques Christoffel and Sylvain Millien, Chefs

Friends in the oil business persuaded Jim Harrigan to come to Houston from Los Angeles in 1971 to open a restaurant. They flew him over Houston in a helicopter until he spotted what he declared was "the" place at Westheimer and Kirby, a major intersection.

Harrigan was the fourth owner of the restaurant and he feels that his operation has been successful because it was remodeled around the customers. "We didn't do any immediate changing of the menu because I wanted to get the feel of the place. When we first opened I was the waiter, I was the busboy and I was the menu, because it was all verbal. Our customers got to know us and they grew with us. We also have stability of personnel.

"At one time we had a fifteen-page menu which I typed out and described all the dishes in great detail. Our customers liked that and from that evolved our present menu. It is strong on freshly-made soups, veal, fish and seafood. The Chef's Corner, a surprise selection, changes daily."

The restaurant has evolved into a place serving fine French food with Continental overtones, but it's not classic French. Old brick, dark wood, a heavy-beamed bar with a baby grand piano, red carpeting and pewter plates combine to provide a rich, intimate look.

"My mother was a great cook," says Harrigan. "We used to go to the Pike Place Market in Seattle where all the farmers would bring their produce. My mother had a place where she bought her eggs, her cheese, her vegetables, her meat and her butter. It was one of the great experiences of my life to see all this wonderful fresh food. That's where I got my love of food."

OYSTERS CAPRI

36 raw oysters with half shells
Parsley-Garlic Butter (see below)
Diced red pimento
Freshly grated Parmesan cheese
36 pieces bacon, uncooked, cut into 1-inch squares

1. Place each oyster on well-cleaned oyster shell.
2. Top with 1 tablespoon Parsley-Garlic Butter.
3. Place 5 to 6 pieces pimento on top of Garlic Butter.
4. Sprinkle each oyster with Parmesan cheese to cover.
5. Place 1 square of raw bacon on top.
6. Bake in a 400-degree oven until bacon is cooked to taste.

PARSLEY-GARLIC BUTTER

1 cup butter, softened
3 or 4 cloves garlic, chopped
1/4 cup plus 1 teaspoon fresh finely chopped parsley
1/2 teaspoon salt
Dash of freshly ground black pepper

1. Cream butter until light.
2. Stir in remaining ingredients and mix well until very well blended.
3. Store in an airtight container in the refrigerator.

The treatment of the food means everything whether it's fresh or frozen. American cooks are often bad with vegetables and let them get soggy. I think vegetables should be fresh, but I don't see anything wrong with good quality frozen foods if you know they come from a reputable dealer and you know that your people are going to handle them properly.

HARRIGAN'S

CAJUN GUMBO

This Fish Stock is the same as the one used for Snapper Riviera.

1 whole stalk celery, finely chopped
3 large onions, finely chopped
4 green bell peppers, diced
Butter
1 cup solid all-vegetable shortening
2 cups flour
4 cups diced tomatoes (fresh or canned)
2 bay leaves
1 teaspoon thyme
Pinch of basil
Pinch of oregano
3 tablespoons fresh lemon juice
1 tablespoon Worcestershire sauce
Pinch of ground black pepper
1/2 teaspoon Tabasco sauce
Salt to taste
2 quarts Fish Stock (see below)
8 ounces raw fish, cut up
4 ounces raw peeled shrimp
2 ounces raw scallops

1. In a large pot, sauté celery, onion and peppers in a small amount of butter over low heat. Continue to heat until the vegetables are half cooked.
2. Make a roux (smooth sauce of browned flour and fat) by melting the shortening and combining it with the flour. Stir until smooth. Cook until light golden brown. Stir and watch carefully; do not let it overcook or burn.
3. Add the roux to the vegetables.
4. Add tomatoes and all seasonings.
5. Add the fish stock and simmer for 1 hour.
6. Ten minutes before serving, add the fish, shrimp and scallops. Simmer and serve.

BASIC FISH STOCK

2 slices lemon
2 sprigs parsley
1/4 medium onion, diced
1½ pounds inexpensive whitefish
1/2 cup vermouth
3 peppercorns
1/2 cup cold water

1. Place the lemon, parsley, onion and fish in a 4-quart saucepan.
2. Add vermouth, peppercorns and enough water to cover.
3. Cover the saucepan and bring the mixture to a fast rolling boil. Skim scum from top as it rises.
4. Add 1/2 cup cold water.
5. Bring to a boil, then reduce heat and boil slowly for about 15 minutes, or until the lemon and onion are slightly transparent and the fish flakes easily.
6. Strain thoroughly. To keep a ready supply of stock, pour the liquid into pint jars, seal and freeze immediately.

HARRIGAN'S

SNAPPER RIVIERA

6 (4-ounce) filets of red snapper or other white fish
Basic Fish Stock
5 ounces cooked crabmeat
5 ounces deveined, shelled, cooked shrimp
5 ounces sliced mushrooms
3 tablespoons butter
Hollandaise Sauce (see below)

1. Grease the perforated base of a steamer with butter and place the filets on the buttered surface. Cover pan.
2. Pour enough Basic Fish Stock into the bottom pan of the steamer to fill half way. Place the perforated pan on top and steam for about 15 minutes, or until the filets flake easily when tested with a fork.
3. Remove filets and keep warm on a serving dish.
4. In a bowl, mix crabmeat, shrimp and mushrooms and set aside.
5. Melt the butter in a skillet and add the mushroom-seafood mixture. Sauté over low heat until hot.
6. Top filets with the seafood mixture and cover with Hollandaise Sauce just before serving.

BASIC HOLLANDAISE

After you have finished making your Hollandaise, serve it *warm*—if the sauce is hot it will thicken and curdle. You can keep it perfectly for an hour or more by putting it over a pan of lukewarm water.

1/2 cup butter
4 egg yolks, well-beaten
2 to 2½ tablespoons fresh lemon juice
Pinch of white pepper
1/8 teaspoon salt

1. Melt 2 tablespoons butter in the top of a double boiler, then pour gradually into the beaten egg yolks, stirring constantly.
2. Return egg yolks to the pan and place in or over hot water.
3. Add remaining butter by tablespoons; stir after each tablespoon is added until it is melted.
4. Remove from heat and stir in the lemon juice, pepper and salt.
5. Be careful to avoid cooking the sauce too long, and do not allow it to become too hot, or it will curdle.

NOTE: If sauce curdles, plunge pot into a basin of ice water and whisk sauce until it reforms.

REAL IRISH COFFEE

This is the *real* recipe for Irish Coffee, as invented at Shannon Airport. The brown sugar makes it authentic. Use nine-ounce coffee mugs with handles (glass cups can burn your fingers) and heat the mugs first by pouring in hot water and letting them sit a minute before draining. For a less authentic, but delicious version, you may substitute one-half ounce Kahlúa for brown sugar.

1½ teaspoons heavy dark brown sugar
Hot brewed coffee
1¼ ounces Jameson Irish Whiskey
Fresh whipped cream

1. Put brown sugar in a 9-ounce coffee mug that has been heated. Pour five ounces coffee in and mix well with sugar.
2. Add Irish Whiskey to the coffee mixture.
3. Pour in enough hot coffee to fill the mug.
4. Top with whipped cream and sprinkle brown sugar on top. Serve immediately.

HARRIGAN'S

FETTUCCINE ALL' ALFREDO

A pinch of nutmeg is the intriguing secret to this dish.

6 quarts chicken stock (can be made with bouillon cubes)
4 tablespoons olive oil
2 pounds fettuccine
1/2 pound butter
2 egg yolks
1/2 cup heavy cream
1 cup freshly grated Parmesan cheese
Salt and pepper to taste
Pinch of nutmeg

1. In a large pot, bring the chicken stock to a boil. Add olive oil.
2. Very gently drop in fettuccine and stir with a wooden spoon for a few minutes to separate noodles. Cook at a gentle boil for just a few minutes until *al dente*.
3. Drain fettuccine in a colander and turn into a large heated serving bowl.
4. Cream butter until fluffy. Add egg yolks and cream and beat constantly while adding cheese, a tablespoon at a time. Add cheese mixture to fettuccine and toss gently.
5. Serve on heated plates, topped with freshly ground pepper and a pinch of nutmeg.

NOTE: This makes enough fettuccine for 6 generous servings or 8 medium servings.

CRÊPES MARNIER

2 cups sugar
4 ounces (1 stick) butter
2 cups fresh orange juice
3 tablespoons fresh lemon juice
3 strips orange rind
2 strips lemon rind
12 crêpes
1/4 cup Cointreau
1/4 cup Grand Marnier
1/4 cup cognac

1. In a shallow chafing dish, heat the sugar until it is a light caramel color and liquified. Add butter.
2. Stir in juices and rind.
3. Reduce flame and cook until syrupy.
4. Baste each crêpe generously on both sides and fold into quarters.
5. Add Cointreau, Grand Marnier and cognac.
6. Flame and serve.

Oyster Stew

Shrimp Cocktail with Old-Fashioned Sauce

Stuffed Celery Hearts

Trout Sauté Meunière

Green Salad with Artichokes

Fresh Baked Potato

Hot French Bread   Butter

Orange Slices with Grand Marnier

Wine:
Graves Superieur or Mâcon Blanc

Mrs. Clifton P. Hebert, Owner
Mrs. P. V. Ryan, Manager
Herman Harbert, Chef

Hebert's Ritz is an old Houston tradition. It was founded in 1939 by Clifton P. Hebert, a waiter who came from New Orleans and who served as maître d'hôtel at several Houston hotels and at Kelley's before opening his first effort. Hebert's began as an eleven-stool diner. In 1941, the restaurant was moved to its present location, a turn-of-the-century house with dark paneling, antiques and stained-glass decor. Hebert was raised in New Orleans, but believing that Texans liked steak and potatoes, he was careful to gradually add the fish dishes and sauces that have become trademarks.

"We have people who have been eating here for thirty years and who have never eaten a steak," says Peg Ryan, Hebert's daughter, who took over the restaurant management after her father died about eight years ago. "Rib steaks, of course, are our specialty. We get the meat from Chicago where it's bought especially for us. It's fairly young beef, but not veal, of consistent size and aging. We cut all our own meat. Our steak sauce is added to all the steaks." Hebert's Ritz is known for its wonderful sauces, all great secret recipes.

"Our chef has been with us since 1939," adds Mrs. Ryan. "He went away to war but came back. The salad girl has been here since 1943. Many guests have been coming to the restaurant for three generations, and three generations of the Hebert family help carry on the restaurant's traditions."

1214 McGowen

HEBERT'S RITZ

OYSTER STEW

1½ cups milk
1/2 cup heavy cream
1½ pints oysters and liquid
1/4 teaspoon freshly ground black pepper
Pinch of cayenne pepper
1½ teaspoons salt
3 tablespoons butter
Finely chopped green onions

1. Combine the milk, cream and oyster liquid in a 3-quart saucepan. Warm over low heat.
2. Add the spices and increase heat, bringing the mixture to a boil.
3. Lower heat and add the oysters. When the edges curl, remove from heat.
4. Add butter.
5. Garnish with chopped green onions and serve.

My dad believed in fresh food. If we can't get fresh fish we just don't serve it. We don't put oysters on the menu in the summer because I don't think that they taste as good.

HEBERT'S RITZ

SHRIMP COCKTAIL WITH HEBERT'S OLD-FASHIONED SAUCE

1 pound fresh or thawed frozen shrimp
2 to 3 tablespoons crab-shrimp boil
1/2 cup salt
3 quarts water
1 large lemon, cut up
Old-Fashioned Sauce (see recipe below)

1. Place crab boil, salt, water and lemon in large pot. Bring to a boil and boil for 10 minutes. Add shrimp and cover pot. Turn off heat and let sit for 5 minutes. *Do not overcook.*
2. Drain immediately. Cool, peel and devein the shrimp. Refrigerate until ready to serve.

OLD-FASHIONED SAUCE

1 pint ketchup
3 tablespoons hot horseradish
2 tablespoons Worcestershire sauce

Combine and serve with shrimp.

STUFFED CELERY

1/2 cup blue cheese
2 tablespoons mayonnaise
Lettuce
16 celery hearts or pieces of sliced celery
Pimento-stuffed olives, sliced
Fresh parsley

1. Blend blue cheese with mayonnaise, mashing the cheese until the mixture is smooth.
2. Top each celery heart or stuff pieces with a small spoonful of the mixture.
3. Arrange 4 or 5 pieces per serving on a bed of lettuce. Garnish with sliced olives and parsley and serve.

HEBERT'S RITZ

TROUT SAUTE MEUNIÈRE

The most important ingredient in this recipe is *fresh* fish.

4 fresh trout filets
Paprika, salt and pepper
1 egg beaten with 2 tablespoons water
Flour
Oil
Sauce Meunière (see below)

1. Season filets with paprika, salt and pepper. Dip them into the egg-water mixture and then into the flour.
2. Pan fry the trout in oil. *Do not overcook.* Remove from pan to serving platter.

We buy nothing over a 2½ pound fish. The larger ones are sometimes mealy. My dad taught me long ago that the smaller ones are better.

SAUCE MEUNIÈRE

1 stick butter
4 generous dashes of Worcestershire sauce
Juice of 2 large lemons
4 teaspoons chopped fresh parsley

1. Brown butter in a skillet. Do not burn.
2. Add Worcestershire sauce and blend well.
3. To serve, pour the juice of half a lemon over each serving of cooked fish. Sprinkle parsley over each and top with Sauce Meuniere. Garnish with a lemon slice dipped in paprika, if desired.

HEBERT'S RITZ

GREEN SALAD WITH ARTICHOKES

1 head lettuce, torn into large pieces
1/4 cup chopped fresh parsley
Ground pepper
1 (6½-ounce) jar artichoke hearts packed in oil
Fresh lemon juice
2 dashes Worcestershire sauce
Salt to taste
2 tomatoes, cut into wedges

1. Toss lettuce, parsley and pepper in a large salad bowl.
2. Remove the lid from the artichoke jar and use it to measure lemon juice equal to the oil from the artichoke hearts.
3. Add oil and Worcestershire sauce.
4. Toss together all ingredients except salt and tomatoes.
5. Add salt and garnish with tomato wedges.

Baked potatoes should be served as soon as they are cooked. At Hebert's Ritz potatoes are baked every forty minutes. We *never* bake them in foil and hold them.

ORANGE SLICES WITH GRAND MARNIER

3 oranges
Grand Marnier
Mint leaves

1. Peel and slice oranges about 1/4-inch thick. Arrange in a fan shape on four plates.
2. Pour Grand Marnier (about 1/2 jigger in all) over orange slices.
3. Garnish with mint leaves and serve.

Hugo's Window Box

Dinner for Six

Lobster Bisque

Esquire Salad

Veal Scallopine au Marsala

Fluffy Rice Pilaf

Soufflé Grand Marnier

Flying Dutchman Coffee

Wine:

*With Bisque, Salad and Veal — Alexander Valley
Pinot Chardonnay, 1975
or Jaboulet Vercherre Meursault*

Dick Nelson, General Manager, Hyatt Regency

Joe Mannke, Food and Beverage Director

Peter Lehr, Executive Chef

Hugo's Window Box resembles a glass box jutting out over the atrium and sculpture lobby of the Hyatt Regency Hotel. Decorated in emerald green and gold, the dining area is located on a raised floor to provide a view for the guests. "Nothing is too good or too expensive for Hugo's," says food and beverage director, Joe Mannke. "Our general manager, Dick Nelson, wanted Hugo's to be a first-class show place with excellent food and a relaxing atmosphere."

To accomplish this goal, the waiters and staff attend monthly classes on food preparation and service. "Our success is based on caring. Hugo's is our little hobby and we offer many little touches you won't find in other restaurants; our butter is served in the shape of little swans, chilled forks are provided for the salads, fresh crudities are served in oversized brandy snifters filled with ice, warm wet napkins are offered from abalone shells at the end of the meal and personalized matches are placed on the tables for all of our guests."

Mr. Mannke says that their guests' favorite foods are seafood dishes and salads, especially their spinach salad. "We go to a great deal of trouble to purchase the freshest ingredients from all over the country, something that is very difficult for an independent restaurant to do."

1200 Louisiana

LOBSTER BISQUE

The trick to this recipe is to first flame the lobster in the shell with brandy, then pound the lobster shells in a mortar and return them to the soup.

1 (1½-pound) whole lobster
1/3 cup corn oil
2 ounces brandy
1 small rib celery, chopped
1 small onion, cut into pieces
1 small carrot, cut into pieces
1 clove garlic, chopped
1/2 teaspoon paprika
Salt and pepper to taste
1 tablespoon tomato purée
1/2 teaspoon crushed tarragon or 1 sprig fresh tarragon
1/3 cup rice
1/4 cup Chablis
1 quart chicken bouillon
1/2 pint light cream

1. Sauté the lobster in hot oil until the shell turns light red, then flambe with brandy.
2. Add vegetables and sauté over low heat for 5 minutes.
3. Combine with paprika, salt and pepper to taste.
4. Add tomato purée, tarragon and rice.
5. Add the wine and chicken bouillon and simmer for 10 minutes.
6. Remove the lobster and extract the meat from the tail and claws. Cut the meat into small pieces.
7. Pound the lobster shell in a mortar and return it to the soup.
8. Simmer for 1½ hours, then strain.
9. Combine with the cream and the cut-up lobster meat. Serve.

HUGO'S WINDOW BOX

ESQUIRE SALAD

1 head iceberg lettuce
1 head limestone lettuce
1 avocado, diced or sliced
2 hard-cooked eggs, diced
4 ounces crumbled blue cheese
12 ounces California bay shrimp
Esquire Dressing (see below)

1. Wash and prepare lettuce for salad.
2. Line 6 chilled glass plates with limestone lettuce leaves.
3. Toss salad ingredients gently in a large bowl.
4. Mix with Esquire Dressing and serve chilled.

ESQUIRE DRESSING

1 cup mayonnaise
1/3 cup heavy cream
1 tablespoon prepared mustard
1/4 teaspoon each thyme, savory and white pepper
1/2 onion, finely grated
1 teaspoon salt
1/4 cup cider vinegar
1/4 cup vegetable oil
2 cloves garlic, minced
1/2 cup grated Gruyère cheese
2 chopped anchovies

Place all ingredients in a chilled bowl and blend thoroughly with an electric mixer.

Salad forks must be cold. We keep ours chilled by standing them in little glass flower pots filled with ice.

HUGO'S WINDOW BOX

VEAL SCALLOPINE AU MARSALA

1½ pounds veal, cut into 1½-ounce scallops
1 teaspoon salt
1/2 teaspoon pepper
Paprika
2 tablespoons butter
1/2 pound fresh mushrooms, thinly sliced
2 shallots, chopped
2 scallions, white part only, finely chopped
1/2 cup Marsala
1/2 cup brown gravy
1 cup heavy cream
1 tablespoon fresh chopped parsley
1 tablespoon cornstarch dissolved in 3 tablespoons water

1. Sprinkle salt, pepper and paprika on each scallop.
2. Melt butter in a large frying pan over high heat and sauté veal on both sides.
3. Reduce heat and add mushrooms, shallots, scallions, Marsala and brown gravy.
4. Simmer for 5 minutes, stirring frequently.
5. Remove the veal from the pan and place it on a hot dish.
6. Combine the cream with the gravy and add the chopped parsley. Bring to a boil.
7. Stir in cornstarch which has been dissolved in the water and simmer, stirring, until the sauce is thickened.
8. Pour the sauce over the veal and serve with Fluffy Rice Pilaf.

At Hugo's Window Box we use white meat veal. Our scallopine is prepared in the dining room, as are many of our special items.

HUGO'S WINDOW BOX

FLUFFY RICE PILAF

1 stick (1/2 cup) butter
1 medium onion, very finely chopped
2 cups Uncle Ben's Converted rice
3½ cups chicken broth
1 bay leaf

1. Melt the butter in a heavy skillet.
2. Add the onion and sauté over low heat, being careful not to let it brown.
3. Add the rice and blend it with the butter and onion.
4. Cover the rice with the hot chicken broth and bring it to a boil.
5. Cover the pot and place it in a moderate (350 degree) oven for 20 to 25 minutes.
6. When ready to serve, place pilaf in a hot bowl and separate the grains with a fork.

SOUFFLÉ GRAND MARNIER

3¼ cups milk
1/4 pound butter
2½ cups all-purpose flour
8 egg yolks
4 whole eggs
1 cup Grand Marnier liqueur
Rind of 2 oranges, grated
4 eggs whites
1/2 cup sugar

1. In a heavy saucepan, bring the milk and butter to a boil. Add the flour and stir until well blended.
2. Stir until the mixture is very thick and no longer sticks to the sides of the pan.
3. Remove from heat and add egg yolks, one by one, beating constantly.
4. Continue beating while adding the whole eggs, the Grand Marnier, and the grated orange rind.
5. Preheat oven to 400 degrees.
6. Beat the egg whites until very stiff and add the sugar gradually, beating until the meringue is very firm.
7. Butter six individual souffle dishes and dust them with sugar.
8. Gently combine the meringue with the flour dough and fill the dishes three-fourths full. Bake at 400 degrees until the souffle rises to double its original size. Reduce heat to 350 degrees and bake until done, about 45 minutes in all. Dust with powdered sugar and serve.

FLYING DUTCHMAN COFFEE

1/2 lemon
4 or 5 teaspoons sugar
8 ounces (1 cup) Vandermint liqueur (chocolate Crème de Menthe)
6 cups freshly brewed coffee
6 teaspoons sugar
1/2 cup whipped cream
8 ounces brandy

1. Moisten the rims of stemmed glass goblets (not crystal) with lemon juice and dip them into sugar.
2. Heat in each glass, over open flame, 1½ ounces Vandermint. Ignite.
3. Fill each glass three-fourths full with hot coffee. Sweeten with 1 teaspoon sugar and top with 2 teaspoons whipped cream.
4. In a ladle, heat 1½ ounces brandy for each drink. Ignite and pour the flaming brandy over the cream and coffee.

Our special coffee cart contains coffees from all over the world and our "coffee queen" can prepare almost any kind of coffee you can think of, at your table.

Dinner for Six

Cold Strawberry Soup

Salad Bar

Cognac Steak

Broccoli Quiche

Zucchini Nut Bread

Apple Strudel

Café La Quiche

Wine:

With Soup — Geyser Peak Pinot Chardonnay, 1975
With Steak — Château Pontet-Canet, 1972

Rudy Lechner, Owner

A brightly striped awning, planter boxes and a gazebo-like central dining area give La Quiche its lighthearted, sidewalk cafe atmosphere.

Owner Rudi Lechner has a solid background as a European-trained chef, who began his career at age fourteen as an apprentice in a pastry shop. He worked for the largest restaurant chain in Europe before coming to the States. Lechner came to the Hyatt-Regency in Houston as a food and beverage director when the hotel opened in 1972. "I liked being a manager, but when you like food, you like food. I couldn't stay away. I still spend a lot of time back in the kitchen."

La Quiche came about by accident, he says. "One weekend we were going to a football game and the neighbors got together to make different kinds of quiches. I made a Caesar salad and we had wine. I said 'This is a great meal. I wonder why no one has ever come up with a restaurant just serving quiche?' " He started experimenting with different recipes at the Hyatt. "I developed my own recipes which worked well, and then decided to go on my own with this restaurant.

"What I am trying to accomplish is an informal, brasserie-cafe-gasthaus type of European restaurant where you can drop in any time you like. You don't have to make it a special occasion and you don't have to eat a whole meal. I like to cater to people's moods, to whatever they want—a piece of quiche, a glass of wine or a sandwich. Quiche is not a fancy item. In Europe, it's a peasant food, actually, and is very nutritious.

2501 S. Gessner

COLD STRAWBERRY SOUP

3 cups fresh strawberries, washed and hulled
3/4 cup sugar or to taste
3/4 cup sour cream
3 cups ice water
3/4 cup red wine such as Burgundy
Sour cream and fresh whole berries for garnish

1. Rub berries through a fine sieve or purée in a blender.
2. Add sugar to taste. Add sour cream and mix.
3. Add water and wine and correct the sweetening. Chill.
4. Serve with a dollop of sour cream and garnish with fresh strawberries.

At the beginning, we had only quiche but now we've changed and have added other dishes which might, for example, appeal to men at dinner. For some reason many men think of quiche as a feminine thing.

LA QUICHE

SALAD BAR

***At La Quiche the extensive salad bar includes a variety of fresh vegetables, assorted salad combinations, cheeses, liver pâté, peanuts, and croutons made of fresh toasted zucchini bread. At home you might use a variety of greens with perhaps carrot salad, cheese, peanuts and croutons.

To refresh the greens before every meal, we wash them in a tub of ice water to "wake them up". Drain well and refrigerate. You could refresh them by putting the greens in a strainer with a bowl of ice water underneath. Just remember to drain well!***

CARROT SALAD

1½ cups mayonnaise
2 tablespoons honey
1/4 cup walnuts, chopped
1/4 cup pineapple chunks
2 tablespoons raisins
1 tablespoon fresh lemon juice
3 pounds carrots, peeled and grated

1. Combine mayonnaise with honey, walnuts, pineapple, raisins and lemon juice. Mix well with a whip.
2. Add dressing gradually to carrots until creamy.

LA QUICHE

COGNAC STEAK

6 (12-ounce) rib-eye steaks
Salt
1/2 teaspoon white pepper
1 teaspoon Dijon mustard
3 cloves garlic, crushed
1/2 pound butter
1½ cups sliced fresh mushrooms
1 tablespoon chopped fresh parsley
3 ounces cognac
3 cups red wine such as Burgundy
Worcestershire sauce
Watermelon and cantaloupe slices, pineapple and strawberries

1. Rub the steaks with salt, pepper, mustard and garlic.
2. Brown the butter in a skillet. Place steaks in butter and sear. Add mushrooms and parsley and reduce by cooking for a few minutes.
3. Flambé with 1 ounce of cognac. Add the red wine.
4. Remove steaks when they have been cooked to desired degree. Reduce the sauce again, until smooth.
5. Add the remaining cognac and season the sauce to taste with salt, pepper, and Worcestershire sauce. Return the steaks to the sauce for a few minutes to heat.
6. To serve, place the steaks on warmed plates and cover each with sauce. Add slices of watermelon, cantaloupe, pineapple and strawberries. Serve with a slice of Broccoli Quiche.

LA QUICHE

ABOUT QUICHE

***I have developed my own technique and recipes for quiche. Each one is broken into three elements—the crust, the filling and the mix. Our quiches are heavier than the usual recipe because we use greater amounts of cheese and eggs and then fill an eight-inch form with nine ounces of mixture. Don't use more than this amount of mixture, or the ingredients won't bind together to produce a nice texture.

We make a basic custard mixture of eggs and milk (or sometimes half and half or heavy cream) and pour that over the filling (half cheese, half vegetables, meat, seafood or whatever). The meat and vegetables should be very cold when you combine them with the custard. Be careful about overcooking vegetables, also. We don't cook zucchini, tomatoes or mushrooms or other vegetables that contain a lot of moisture but instead, add them raw.

Our crust has less liquid in it so it doesn't get soggy. We put in the cold filling, then pour the custard mix over that and bake for about 40 minutes at a fairly high temperature of 400 degrees. Then we cover the quiche with a foil pan and bake 10 minutes more. At home you should cut the temperature to about 350 or 375 degrees. Bake the quiche until it is slightly set and firm; it should have no color. Then cover and bake for 10 minutes.***

Quiche is almost a fast food item in Europe. Except for the onion quiche, vegetable quiches are American inventions. All varieties, vegetable and otherwise, are very nutritious.

BROCCOLI QUICHE

These are beautiful when they cook—just like a soufflé. All the quiches, except the dessert type, are served with a cheese sauce, essentially a Bechamel with white wine.

6 eggs
3/4 cup milk or half and half
Dash of salt and white pepper
Dash of nutmeg
8 ounces fresh broccoli
5 ounces grated Cheddar cheese
Sprinkle of Chablis wine
1 (9-inch) unbaked pie shell

1. Blanch, chop and drain broccoli. Chill.
2. Mix the eggs and half and half. Add salt, pepper and nutmeg.
3. Place the broccoli and cheese in the pie shell. Sprinkle with wine.
4. Pour the egg mixture over the broccoli.
5. Bake for 50 minutes at 375 degrees. Cover the top of the quiche with foil or an inverted foil pan during the last 10 minutes of baking. Test to see if it is done by inserting a silver knife in the center. It should come out clean, but *do not* let quiche bake too long or it will be too dry.

Our newspaper-style menu was developed as a means of educating the public about our product. Our break-down of ingredients lets people know what they're eating, how many calories, how much protein, etc. We plan to have similar descriptions of our other foods.

LA QUICHE

ZUCCHINI NUT BREAD

This is one of the most popular items on the menu at La Quiche. Leftover bread is lightly toasted to make croutons for the salad.

5 eggs
1½ cups oil
2 teaspoons vanilla
1 tablespoon lemon juice
1¼ cups sugar
3 cups flour
1 teaspoon salt
1 tablespoon cinnamon
1½ teaspoons baking powder
2 teaspoons baking soda
1/3 cup chopped nuts
1/4 cup raisins
3/4 pound finely grated zucchini
Egg wash (1 whole egg mixed with 1/4 cup milk)

1. Preheat oven to 350 degrees. Combine the eggs, oil, vanilla and lemon juice.
2. In a separate bowl, mix sugar, flour, salt, cinnamon, baking powder, baking soda, nuts, raisins and zucchini.
3. Gradually add the dry ingredients to the liquid. Beat until smooth.
4. Grease and flour two (9x5x3-inch) loaf pans. Divide the mixture evenly between them. Bake at 350 degrees for 50 minutes.
5. When the bread is nearly done, brush the top with the egg wash and return to oven until done.

At La Quiche, the zucchini bread is baked in pie pans. The bread can be frozen successfully. For best results, leave it in foil and reheat in a 350-degree oven for about 20 to 25 minutes.

APPLE STRUDEL

In Vienna, everyone learns to make strudel at home. The recipe is just a guideline; you must have a *feel* for the dough. It can't be too soft, but if it's too firm, it won't stretch. If you wish, you can use phyllo pastry.

DOUGH

1/2 pound (2 cups) flour
1 egg
1 tablespoon oil
1/4 teaspoon salt
3/4 cup lukewarm water (about)

1. Place the flour on a counter or butcher's block. Make a well in the center and add the egg, oil and salt. Mix with fingers from the center out. Add water slowly until the dough is firm.
2. Knead the dough very well until it is soft, but firm and smooth. Form into a round and place in a floured bowl.
3. Slightly cover the dough with oil. Let dough rest at least 30 minutes at room temperature.
4. Place a tablecloth or cover on a large work area or dining table. Sprinkle lightly with flour and place dough in the center of the cloth.
5. Pull the dough at the edges first to enlarge the circle. Flour your hands and begin pulling the dough lightly from underneath from all angles with the back of your hands. *Be very careful that the dough doesn't break.* When the dough is pulled out, it should be paper thin.

LA QUICHE

FILLING

3 pounds tart apples such as Winesaps, peeled, cored and thinly sliced
Fine dry bread crumbs ("French bread is good")
Cinnamon to taste
1/2 cup sugar
Raisins, as desired
1/4 cup chopped walnuts
1/4 pound melted butter
Egg wash (1 whole egg mixed with 1/4 cup milk)
Powdered sugar
Whipped cream

1. Pour melted butter over the strudel dough. Sprinkle with bread crumbs.
2. Place the sliced apples on top. Sprinkle evenly with the sugar, cinnamon, raisins and walnuts.
3. Pull dough over the table edge, then trim off the thick edges all the way around.
4. Fold the long edge over and roll the strudel up to form a long roll. Fold like a horseshoe shape on a pan, then flip upside down onto a buttered cookie sheet. Bake at 350 degrees until golden brown, about 1 hour. Brush dough with the egg wash periodically while baking to prevent crust from becoming too dry. Cover strudel with aluminum foil the last 10 minutes of baking.
5. Serve the strudel warm, sprinkled with powdered sugar and a tablespoon of whipped cream.

CAFÉ LA QUICHE

Per person:

1/2 ounce Irish whiskey
1/2 ounce Kahlúa
Hot coffee
Whipped cream
1/2 ounce Galliano liqueur

1. In a coffee mug, pour whiskey and Kahlúa and fill with hot coffee to about 1 inch below the rim.
2. Top with a spoonful of whipped cream.
3. Gently float 1/2 ounce Galliano on cream. Serve with a straw.

Dinner for Six

Redfish Court Bouillon à la Louisiane

Tomatoes Camille

Fresh Jumbo Asparagus

Breast of Chicken Camille

Crème Brulée or Chocolate Mousse

Wine:

With Dinner — Antonin Rodet Meursault, 1975

With or After Dessert — Barsac

Camille Bermann, Owner

Jesus M. Davila, Executive Chef

"I was Escoffier's last student," says Camille Bermann, owner of Maxim's, a Houston landmark. Bermann worked with the famous Henri Soule at the New York World's Fair in 1939 and came to Houston via the Beverly Country Club in New Orleans. In 1950 he opened the original Maxim's. The restaurant has been in its present downtown location since 1958.

Walls of the red plush and gilt restaurant are decorated with oversized French Impressionist prints. Several walls display the restaurant's and the owner's many awards, including the Order du Merite Agricole from the French Ministry of Agriculture and a coveted gold Escoffier medal. Displays of fresh fruit and vegetables in the entry greet guests. Fresh flowers and starched white clothes adorn each table.

Maxim's kitchen is relatively small. Bermann doesn't like to use anything but fresh foods, so there is limited storage. Two butchers cut all the meat and fresh fish.

Bermann says that people know more about good food now because "the world has become very small; everybody travels so much. Now people tell the chef how they want to have something cooked." He believes that fine cooking requires fresh ingredients, skill, and time and that a restaurateur is one of a special breed, "not crazy, but a little like a gypsy". His son, Ronnie, also in the business, apprenticed in Europe where he even learned how to make wine at Chateau Lascombes.

"We have foundation," says Bermann. "About seventy-five per cent of my help has been with me for twenty years or more. I think the restaurant is successful because the harder I work, the luckier I get. I never stop trying to make Maxim's the best restaurant in the world."

802 Lamar at Milam

MAXIM'S

REDFISH COURT BOUILLON A LA LOUISIANE

When adding seasonings, remember that this should be on the spicy side.

1 (5 or 6-pound) redfish, cut in 3-inch pieces
2½ quarts cold water
5 cups white wine ("California wine is fine")
1½ cups white wine vinegar
Juice of 2 lemons
1 (12-ounce) can tomato paste
1 bay leaf
3 medium-sized white onions
4 cloves garlic
3 carrots
2 ribs celery
6 sprigs parsley
2 fresh jalapeño peppers
Salt, pepper and Tabasco sauce to taste

1. Combine cold water, wine, vinegar, lemon juice, tomato paste and bay leaf. Poach fish.
2. Finely chop onion, garlic, carrots, celery, parsley and jalapeños. (*Seed peppers under cold running water if you don't want a really hot sauce.*)
3. Combine fish, poaching liquid and chopped vegetables in a large pot. Bring to a rolling boil. Simmer for 20 minutes.
4. Season to taste with salt, pepper and Tabasco sauce.

When you have ten pounds of meat, it's easy to make good soup for two people, but when you have no meat, that's the test. I practice Escoffier's rules; he is my law. So long as I have pepper, salt, onions and carrots, a little garlic, white wine and butter, I don't care what it is, I can cook it. My son, Ronnie, can do the same thing. At Maxim's we are professionals.

TOMATOES CAMILLE

6 medium tomatoes, peeled and sliced
1/2 onion, finely chopped
4 tablespoons chopped fresh parsley
Dressing (see below)

1. Place sliced tomatoes on a cold plate. Cover with onions and parsley.
2. Top with dressing.

DRESSING

3 teaspoons mustard
2/3 cup oil
1/3 cup vinegar
Salt and pepper to taste
2 cloves garlic, chopped finely
Juice of 1/2 lemon
2 tablespoons Worcestershire sauce

Blend ingredients well.

This is a delicious way to serve tomatoes.

FRESH JUMBO ASPARAGUS

***This can serve as an excellent first course or as a vegetable accompanying the entrée. Green jumbo asparagus don't have to be trimmed like the white asparagus because the green are less woody. At Maxim's we trim only about half an inch from the bottom.

After it's cooked, we put a towel around the asparagus so they won't break.***

24 spears fresh jumbo asparagus
Boiling salted water
Lemon butter or Hollandaise sauce

1. Bring salted water to a boil in a large pot. Drop in asparagus. When water returns to the boil, cook for about 5 minutes. Drain.
2. Drop asparagus into bowl of cool water or let water run from faucet over them.
3. To serve, reheat the asparagus in a fresh pot of boiling water. Drain and serve with lemon butter or Hollandaise at the table.

To prepare a good Hollandaise, keep in mind that the butter should not be hot to the touch when you add it to the sauce. To keep the sauce at the proper temperature, add a little cracked ice, then the melted butter, and beat constantly with a wire whip.

BREAST OF CHICKEN CAMILLE

You can do so much with one chicken. From a 2½ pound capon, you have the two breasts for one dish. The two legs make chicken fried steak (cut out the bone in the middle and flatten the meat with a cleaver.) The chicken livers can be prepared en brochette or lightly sautéed. Chop up the gizzards in rice and serve as a side dish or mixed with wild rice. You can fry the wings as an hors d'oeuvres. The bones go to make onion soup or in chicken stock. *Be sure to have the oven really hot for this recipe.*

6 single chicken breasts
Flour, salt and pepper
1/4 cup cooking oil
3 or 4 tablespoons butter
1/2 cup chopped shallots
1 clove garlic, finely chopped
5 tablespoons chopped fresh parsley
1¼ cups sliced fresh mushrooms
1/2 cup—or slightly more—dry white wine
1/2 cup consommé
Cooked wild rice

1. Season chicken with salt and pepper and dredge lightly in flour.
2. Heat oil in a large skillet. Brown chicken and cook over low heat until tender. Remove from skillet and pour off excess oil.
3. Add butter, stirring to loosen drippings in bottom of pan. Add shallots, garlic and parsley. Saute over low heat.
4. Add mushrooms and saute 10 minutes.
5. Add wine and consomme (about 1¼ cups liquid in all). Cook for 10 minutes.
6. To serve, place one chicken breast over cooked wild rice and cover with mushroom sauce.

Ladies, prepare a meal as a general prepares a battle. There are no good ten minute dinners—no such thing.

CRÈME BRULÉE

(Caramel Custard)

3 cups half-and-half
7 egg yolks
1/3 cup sugar
1 tablespoon vanilla extract
1/4 cup sifted brown sugar

1. Heat cream in top of a double boiler. Beat yolks, adding sugar gradually, until thick.
2. Slowly add heated cream to egg-sugar mixture. Add vanilla.
3. Pour the mixture into 1½-quart glass baking dish; place in a pan of hot water. Bake in a preheated 325-degree oven for about 1 hour or until set.
4. Let custard cool for about 1 hour.
5. Sift the brown sugar over the custard and place it under the broiler until the sugar melts.
6. Chill until very cold.

CHOCOLATE MOUSSE

5 ounces semisweet chocolate bits
2 tablespoons water
2 tablespoons instant coffee
5 eggs, separated
1/4 cup sugar
1/2 pint whipping cream

1. In a double boiler, melt together the chocolate, water and coffee (dissolved in water). Stir occasionally until smooth. Cool.
2. Pour the mixture into an electric mixer. Add the egg yolks, one at a time, beating continuously.
3. In a second bowl, beat the egg whites, adding sugar gradually, until stiff. Fold the whites into the first mixture.
4. Whip the cream and fold it into the mixture.
5. Spoon the mousse into individual glass dishes. Refrigerate for at least 3 hours.

Dinner for Six

Frozen Margaritas

Guacamole Salad

Carne Guisada, Green Enchiladas

Dips: Chili con Queso, Red Sauce

Garnish: Pico de Gallo

Serve with Mexican Beer

Ninfa Laurenzo, Owner

"Lots of people don't get excited about cooking, but I do," says Ninfa Laurenzo, whose restaurant success has been called mind boggling. Ninfa opened her first restaurant in 1973. That ten-tabled cafe grew into four restaurants with a two million dollar annual payroll and a staff of 500 persons. Ninfa's restaurants are known worldwide. All feature as a logo a big parrot who is saying "gracias". The parrot is displayed on the walls, billboards, menus and waiters' name tags. Says Ninfa, "The parrot is a symbol of love and Christmas and somehow, we've been able to project love in whatever we've done."

The restaurants are a full family affair; the five Laurenzo children, brothers and sisters-in-law, nieces and nephews all share the work. Ninfa came to Houston in 1948 and, with her husband, started a food company that produced Mexican tortillas, taco shells, and Italian bread. Now she is chairman of Ninfa's Tacos al Carbon Inc.

The restaurant's recipes are a combination of what she learned from her mother and what was learned by traveling through Mexico. "When we started, people said that our food would never sell, but we were serving *real* Mexican food and the public liked it. We cook what we eat at home. If you can't eat the food, then you don't want anybody else to eat it.

"We expand our menu by experimenting with old recipes and we try to appeal to all groups of diners. My work is exciting and very satisfying. What else can you say but thanks to people who stand in line to come eat at your restaurants?"

2704 Navigation
6154 Westheimer
9333-B Katy Freeway (Echo Lane)
8507 Gulf Freeway

FROZEN MARGARITAS

8 ounces freshly squeezed lime or lemon juice (preferably lime)
12 ounces Triple Sec liqueur
6 ounces tequila
Crushed ice
Lime wedges
Salt

1. Combine all ingredients except lime wedges and salt in a blender, using enough crushed ice to form a slush-like consistency.
2. Moisten the rim of each cocktail glass with a lime wedge and dip the glass into a plate of salt to give a nice rim of salt around the edge.
3. Pour the Margarita mixture into the glass and squeeze a lime wedge over the top of the drink. Drop the rind into the glass and serve.

In cooking, it is always possible to buy many things already prepared but your end product will never taste as good as it does when everything is freshly prepared.

Our sauces are different from what you find elsewhere. They are all family recipes. When cooking Mexican food, remember that the *real* secret is in the sauce.

GUACAMOLE SALAD

4 well-ripened avocados
1 large ripe tomato, peeled
1 teaspoon salt
1/2 teaspoon garlic powder
1 tablespoon olive oil
Juice of 1/4 lemon

1. Peel avocados. Chop and then mash them to a pulp.
2. Dice the tomato and add it to the avocados along with the remaining seasonings.
3. Add lemon juice and blend thoroughly.

This menu represents what we serve at our restaurants—*real* Mexican food, not Tex-Mex.

All tortillas are not the same. Factory tortillas never taste as good as homemade ones. At Ninfa's *every* tortilla is made by hand. The secret is to add *hot* water to the mixture until you have the proper consistency.

CARNE GUISADA

1½ pounds chopped sirloin
1/2 cup cherry wine
1½ teaspoons salt
1 cup cooking oil
1/2 teaspoon garlic
1/4 teaspoon cominos (cumin seeds)
1/4 teaspoon pepper
1 tablespoon tomato paste
1 tablespoon beef broth concentrate
1/4 tomato
1/4 onion
1/2 bell pepper, sliced
Juice of about 1/2 lemon

1. Sauté chopped sirloin with wine and salt in oil over low heat until brown and tender. Drain excess fat.
2. Combine the garlic, cominos, pepper, tomato paste, beef broth concentrate, tomato and onion in a blender. Blend for 2 minutes.
3. Add to the cooked meat mixture. Cook over low heat for about 15 more minutes.
4. As it continues to simmer, arrange bell pepper slices over top of meat. Remove from heat.
5. Add a few drops lemon juice and serve.

In cooking, the personal touch is very important.

GREEN ENCHILADAS

2 pounds pork roast
2 jalapeno peppers, fried in oil
4 green tomatoes (fresadilla), boiled until tender
1/4 teaspoon garlic
1/4 teaspoon salt
1 tablespoon sour cream
Lard (solid animal fat)
1 egg
12 tortillas

1. Prepare pork roast by boiling it with garlic and salt to taste. When done, chop finely.
2. Place jalapenos, green tomatoes, garlic, salt and sour cream in blender and blend well.
3. Heat 1/3 cup lard in a saucepan. Remove ingredients from the blender and fry in hot lard.
4. Beat egg. Remove the sauce from the heat and quickly add the egg, stirring well.
5. Heat in additional 1/2 cup lard. Dip the tortillas in the sauce and then in the melted hot lard.
6. Stuff the tortillas with the chopped pork mixture.
7. Place on a large platter. Continue until each tortilla has been dipped into the enchilada sauce, then into lard, then stuffed with the pork.
8. When all the enchiladas are prepared, cover them with the remaining sauce and serve.

CHILI CON QUESO

2 cups whole milk
1 (2-pound) loaf Velveeta cheese, cut into small chunks
3 jalapeno peppers, chopped
1 small tomato, chopped
1 tablespoon chopped fresh cilantro (coriander)
1/2 cup chopped bell pepper

1. Bring milk to a boil over medium heat, being careful not to scorch.
2. Add cheese and stir until it is completely dissolved into a thick, creamy consistency.
3. Add remaining chopped ingredients.
4. Remove from heat. Let stand about 10 minutes before serving.

RED SAUCE

5 tomatoes
1 teaspoon salt
2 Arbol chilies (fried in oil)
2 Serrano chilies
1 tablespoon chopped cilantro (coriander)
1/2 teaspoon garlic

1. Boil tomatoes until tender. Remove from heat and place in blender.
2. Add remaining ingredients and blend until you achieve the desired consistency—a thick, delicious sauce.

PICO DE GALLO

5 tomatoes, peeled and very finely chopped
1 small onion, very finely chopped
1 tablespoon cilantro (coriander)
Juice of 1/2 lemon
1/2 teaspoon salt

1. Mix tomato, onion and chopped cilantro.
2. Add lemon juice and salt.

Dinner for Six

Fried Eggplant Appetizer

Fresh Spinach and Squash Soup with Orange

*Roast Leg of Lamb with Garlic and Rosemary,
Artichokes and Hollandaise Sauce
or Greek Lemon Sauce*

French Bread   Butter

Vanilla Mousse

Wine:

With Appetizer and Soup — Bertani Soave

With Lamb — St. Emilion

*With Dessert — Freixenet Cordon Negro Sparkling
Wine from Spain*

Elouise Hetherly, Owner

Food served in a nostalgic setting with wooden tables, cane back chairs, ceiling fans and a blackboard menu keeps bringing fans back to Ouisie's Table from the surrounding neighborhood—the Texas Medical Center, Rice University and the Museum of Fine Arts.

Owner Elouise Hetherly may have such exotica on the menu as Cornish game hens stuffed with tamales or cream of lettuce soup, but it's understood that best-selling items, pimento cheese and egg salad, are always available. In fact, the table for Ouisie's third birthday party displayed the house pâté at one end and a pimento cheese ring at the other. What can be so outstanding about egg salad or pimento cheese? Apparently, that's Ouisie's secret.

The restaurant is in the former Sunset Food Market, which also enjoyed loyal neighborhood trade. The Store-side opened first to bring in revenue while the restaurant got underway. Here, the diner can find the latest whimseys from appliquéd pillows, handmade dolls and valentines to Kliban Cat Calendars. Tobin Haynes built the bar and sculptured woodwork and arches.

The restaurant has been enlarged to accommodate seventy-five, with twelve places available at a big round community table. "You can tell a lot about people's personalities by who will sit there and who won't," says Hetherly. "At first, people were reluctant to sit down with strangers but it's wonderful to see how they've warmed up to the idea. Now we have lots of regulars.

Fresh is the cardinal rule at Ouisie's; it doesn't even have a freezer. With few exceptions, the menu changes daily. Recipes are tested at home before being added to the menu. Currently, Tuesdays are Chicken Fried Steak nights with corn pudding, with greens and black-eyed peas sharing the menu. Thursdays or Fridays are likely to be curry nights and the rest of the dinner menus are at the owner's whim.

1708 Sunset

FRIED EGGPLANT APPETIZER

If your guests really like eggplant, one won't be enough. Keep adding oil, little by little, to the skillet because the eggplant is just like a sponge. I like the taste of olive oil with the vegetable. We prefer an Italian olive oil; it should be hot, but not smoking.

1 large eggplant, or 2 medium
Salt and pepper
Yellow cornmeal
Hot oil for frying

1. Wash eggplant and slice it in 1/4-inch rounds. *Do not peel.*
2. Salt and pepper each slice and dip in cornmeal.
3. Fry in hot oil in a skillet, a few slices at a time. Keep adding oil, little by little, as necessary.
4. Drain on paper towels and serve.

FRESH SPINACH AND SQUASH SOUP WITH ORANGE

This unusual combination of ingredients and flavors make a rich, but refreshing soup. The secret is using all fresh vegetables and clarified butter. Fresh mint makes a wonderful addition.

1/2 cup chopped green onions
Clarified butter
1/2 cup fresh mushrooms, sliced
4 small young yellow squash
1 (10 or 12-ounce) bag fresh spinach, washed, stemmed and torn
1 cup fresh orange juice
1/4 cup fresh lemon juice
1 teaspoon grated orange rind
1/2 teaspoon grated lemon rind
2 quarts rich, flavorful chicken stock ("Be sure it's not watery!")
Salt
Freshly ground pepper
1/2 teaspoon nutmeg
1 teaspoon marjoram
Fresh mint (optional)

1. Sauté the green onions in clarified butter. Add mushrooms and cook together for 2 to 3 minutes.
2. Add the squash. Turn frequently to glaze the squash on all sides. Cook over high heat. When softened, add spinach.
3. When the spinach wilts, add orange and lemon juice and grated rinds. Bring to a simmer and simmer for 2 to 3 minutes.
4. Add the chicken stock and bring the mixture to a boil. Reduce heat to a simmer and check seasoning.
5. Add salt to taste, plus pepper, nutmeg, marjoram, and (if desired) fresh mint.

ROAST LEG OF LAMB WITH GARLIC AND ROSEMARY, ARTICHOKES, AND HOLLANDAISE SAUCE OR GREEK LEMON SAUCE

1 leg of lamb, boned and tied
Garlic, rosemary, salt and pepper
2 large yellow onions, thinly sliced
Olive oil
2 (14-ounce) cans artichoke hearts, drained and quartered
Fresh lemon juice
Melted butter
Freshly grated Parmesan cheese
Blender Hollandaise Sauce or Greek Lemon Sauce (see below)
Rice

1. Roast the lamb using plenty of garlic, rosemary, salt and pepper. Place lamb on a rack in a roasting pan and roast at 325 degrees for 30 minutes per pound. A meat thermometer should register 135 to 140 degrees for medium-done.
2. Sauté the onions in olive oil and spread them over the lamb. When cooked to desired state, let the lamb "rest" and make pan juices by adding water to the scrapings in the pan. Season to taste.
3. Place drained, quartered artichokes in a baking dish. Sprinkle with lemon juice and melted butter, salt, pepper and Parmesan cheese. Cover with foil and bake at 350 degrees until very hot.
4. Slice the lamb and serve it over rice with some of the pan juices. Top with artichokes, cover with lemon sauce or Hollandaise sauce, and sprinkle with a little finely chopped parsley. Serve with hot French bread and some of the sauce and pan juices for the table.

BLENDER HOLLANDAISE SAUCE

2 egg yolks
1 stick (1/4 pound) butter, melted
3 tablespoons fresh lemon juice
Dash of cayenne pepper

1. Blend the egg yolks in a blender. Add melted butter in a stream while blending continuously.
2. Add lemon juice and cayenne to taste and blend thoroughly.

GREEK LEMON SAUCE

This will be a thinner sauce than the Hollandaise. The hot broth called for can be made from the lamb leg bone, while the lamb is roasting. Cover the bone with water and add bay leaf, salt, crushed peppercorns, a carrot, celery, onion, etc. for seasoning.

3 eggs
Juice of 2 lemons, strained
1 cup hot broth

1. Beat the eggs in a blender until thick and light yellow. Add the lemon juice slowly.
2. Add the hot broth slowly to prevent the eggs from curdling.

VANILLA MOUSSE

If you prefer almond flavor, use almond extract in place of vanilla and Amaretto instead of Tia Maria or Kahlúa. A few toasted almonds sprinkled on top gives a nice texture contrast to the smoothness of the mousse.

1 pint heavy cream
1/2 cup sugar
1 teaspoon vanilla extract
2 egg whites
Tia Maria or Kahlúa liqueur

1. Whip the cream to a peak, adding sugar gradually. Add vanilla.
2. Beat the egg whites until stiff and carefully fold them into the cream.
3. Refrigerate until well chilled and spoon into glasses when ready to serve, making little valleys and peaks.
4. Drizzle Tia Maria or Kahlúa over top and around sides.

the RIVOLI

Dinner for Six

Avocado Soup

Spinach Salad

Chicken Calvados

Strawberry Torte

Wine:

With Meal — Weingut Kloftermuhle Ockfener Bockstein, 1976 or Château Kressman La Tour Martillac, 1975

After Dinner — Hine V.S.O.P. Cognac

Willie Rometsch and Ed Zielinsky, Owners

Gunther Hoffman, Executive Chef

The Rivoli, a relative newcomer to Houston, already is one of the most talked-about restaurants in the city. Owner Willie Rometsch, a chef who helped to establish eleven of the most successful restaurants in Houston, now concentrates on the Rivoli exclusively. His partner is Ed Zielinsky, who came from New York where he owned the Grenadier and was associated with several successful clubs, including Raffles.

A recent expansion has doubled the size of The Rivoli's kitchen. "Now we can prepare in the proper manner, the kind of food we want to serve," says Zielinsky. Menu emphasis is veal, fresh fish, and fresh vegetables.

"We started with a casual approach but have gone more formal." Wooden latticework walls in a soothing brown, a lush garden terrace, private wine room, piano bar and backgammon area provide the ambiance. The extensive menu is Continental leaning heavily to French.

"Houstonians know food," says Zielinsky. "They now have more free time to spend on dining. He believes that increased travel also makes a difference. "Houston is like New York was in the 1950's. People here love all the flash, the flambés and the fancy desserts. New Yorkers, however, are always on the run. You can pass food off to a New Yorker pretty easily. Houstonians may spend an entire evening at dinner."

5636 Richmond

THE RIVOLI

AVOCADO SOUP

6 avocados
Salt, white pepper and fresh lemon juice to taste
2 cups cold chicken velouté
2 cups sour cream

1. Make chicken velouté by adding a paste of 1 tablespoon butter and 1 tablespoon flour for each cup of hot chicken stock. Cool velouté.
2. Peel and mash avocados.
3. Add salt, pepper and lemon juice to mashed avocados.
4. Combine the avocado mixture with the velouté.
5. Add sour cream and chill.

Soups such as this one are amongst our most popular items.

THE RIVOLI

SPINACH SALAD

2 pounds leaf spinach
Salad Dressing (see below)
12 fresh white mushrooms, sliced
4 ounces cooked, chopped bacon
3 hard-cooked eggs
12 cherry tomatoes

1. Clean, wash and drain the spinach well. Place in a bowl and add salad dressing. Mix gently but thoroughly.
2. Serve on salad plates and sprinkle generously with mushrooms, bacon, chopped egg whites and chopped egg yolks.
3. Garnish with 2 cherry tomatoes each.

SALAD DRESSING

4 tablespoons prepared mustard
1 tablespoon English mustard
5 ounces white vinegar
4 ounces salad oil
Dash of ground cominos (cumin seed)
Salt and pepper to taste

1. Combine all ingredients. Chill in the refrigerator before using.

THE RIVOLI

CHICKEN CALVADOS

6 boned breasts of chicken, pounded flat
Salt

Stuffing:
3 ounces butter
3 ounces diced apples (preferably Washington State)
2 ounces chopped almonds
4 ounces crumbled cornbread
1/2 ounce Calvados

Brown sauce

1. Salt chicken lightly.
2. To make stuffing, brown butter in skillet and add apples and almonds. Blend in the crumbled cornbread and Calvados. Mix to a paste.
3. Spread stuffing on the bone side of the chicken breast and form into an oval shape.
4. Sauté the breasts in butter until done.
5. Serve with brown sauce.

THE RIVOLI

STRAWBERRY TORTE

1 (8-inch) round sponge cake
3 ounces Kirschwasser (clear cherry brandy)
Butter Frosting (see below)
2 pints strawberries, hulled and cut in half
6 whole strawberries for garnish

1. Cut cake twice horizontally to make 3 layers.
2. Make Butter Frosting.
3. Sprinkle the three cake layers with Kirsch and spread with frosting.
4. Arrange strawberries on top of two layers and then cover the berries with more Butter Frosting. Stack the layers.
5. Cover sides with frosting.
6. Mark six portions and garnish each piece with a whole strawberry or a rosette of whipped cream and a strawberry.
7. Refrigerate until chilled, then cut.

THE RIVOLI

BUTTER FROSTING

1½ cups sweet butter
9 cups powdered sugar, sifted
12 tablespoons (3/4 cup) whipping cream
2 teaspoons vanilla
2 ounces Kirsch

1. Cream butter. Add remaining ingredients and continue creaming until mixture is well blended and fluffy.

Our strawberry torte is always fresh. Whipped cream cakes should never sit for a long time in the refrigerator.

Rudi's...

Dinner for Four

Crabmeat Maison

French Onion Soup Gratinée

Tomatoes Niçoise

Veal Piccata

Fudge Pecan Ball

Wine:

With Crabmeat, Soup and Veal — Pouilly-Fuissé or Bernkasteler Graben Dr. Thanisch

Alternate for Veal — Château Gloria, 1971

Joe Lucia, Owner

Denny Dorsch, Executive Chef

Rudi's has remained an "in" restaurant through a succession of owners since it opened sixteen years ago.

Recently redecorated, it greets guests in a dramatic, artistic way with handwrought sculpture-like silver and brass doors by Tom Wheeler. The soothing, but striking decor continues throughout with wine-colored suede walls as a foil for paintings, wine suede banquettes and niches holding brass containers of stylized flowers.

The restaurant offers Continental cuisine.

"I think of Rudi's as a festive restaurant," says owner Joe Lucia. "You can really linger and enjoy eating; there's no hurry. I come from a family of good cooks and I like to have people treated in my restaurant the way I like to be treated when I go out."

In Fashion Square
on South Post Oak Road

CRABMEAT MAISON

1 cup lump crabmeat
1/4 cup butter
1 green onion, chopped
1/2 cup sliced mushrooms
Almond halves
Chablis
4 artichoke bottoms
1 cup medium cream sauce made with half-and-half and cream
Salt and pepper
Freshly grated Parmesan cheese

1. Sauté crabmeat in butter with the green onion, mushrooms and almonds. Add a generous splash of Chablis and cook until the crab is soft.
2. Divide the mixture into fourths and place some on each artichoke bottom.
3. Top with cream sauce and a sprinkling of Parmesan cheese.

If your white sauce is hot enough, the Parmesan cheese will melt nicely into the mixture when served.

RUDI'S

FRENCH ONION SOUP GRATINEE

4 onions (about 1½ pounds), sliced
Butter (about 1/4 cup)
4 or 5 cups good beef stock
2 cups Chablis
White pepper and salt to taste
4 toast rounds
4 slices Swiss cheese

1. Peel the onions and slice thinly. Sauté in butter until yellow.
2. Add the stock and bring it to a boil. Skim grease as it rises to the top.
3. Add the wine, white pepper and salt to taste and simmer for about 30 minutes.
4. Place a toast round and one slice of cheese into individual bowls or casseroles. Pour hot soup over the top to melt the cheese. Serve.

TOMATOES NIÇOISE

Romaine lettuce
8 slices tomato
8 slices avocado
4 artichoke hearts
Rudi's Vinaigrette Dressing (see below)

1. On a base of romaine, layer two slices of tomato and two slices of avocado topped with an artichoke heart.
2. Add Rudi's Vinaigrette Dressing.

RUDI'S VINAIGRETTE DRESSING

Oil
Water
Red wine vinegar
Salt and pepper

1. Blend equal portions of oil, water and vinegar.
2. Season and shake well.

VEAL PICCATA

This is one of the restaurant's trademark dishes. The secret is getting good veal and treating it gently.

8 (3-ounce) veal cutlets
Flour (about 1/2 cup)
1/4 cup butter
2 tablespoons dry white wine
2 tablespoons fresh lemon juice
1 tablespoon freshly chopped parsley

1. Dust veal with the flour and saute in butter.
2. Add wine, lemon juice and parsley and simmer for about 5 minutes. Serve immediately.

FUDGE PECAN BALL

4 large scoops homemade-type vanilla ice cream
Chopped pecans
Chocolate syrup
Whipped cream

1. Roll ice cream in chopped pecans and freeze.
2. Place ice cream in a dessert dish and top with pecans and chocolate syrup.
3. Garnish with whipped cream and serve.

We recommend using Hershey's chocolate fudge.

ruggles restaurant

Dinner for Six

*Tomatoes Manfred
with Swiss Vinaigrette Dressing*

Snapper Florentine

Judy's Mud Pie

Corduroy Mallet Freeze

Wine:

*With Dinner—Schloss Vollrads Gutenberg, 1973 or
Mâcon Lugny Les Charmes, 1973*

Manfred Jachmich, Owner

Cheow Hwa Yong, Executive Chef

Ruggles is one of the continuing successes of Westheimer's restaurant row. It was opened in 1974 by Manfred Jachmich, who comes from a restaurant family in Koblenz, Germany, and who apprenticed and trained in Germany and Switzerland.

Jachmich came to the U.S. in 1963 when he was twenty-three, and was part of the first crew that opened Hotel America (now the Whitehall) in Houston. He worked for various restaurants and hotels, attended college, became manager and partner in the Bismarck when it was owned by Willie Rometsch, and then owned his own restaurant, Oliver's.

"When I opened Ruggles, antique shops, stained glass and the quaint look were very much in vogue on Westheimer." Ruggles was designed by Don Bolen and was geared to the New Orleans look and its cuisine. Fresh fish and seafood and beignets were prominent on the menu. The menu has developed in a more Continental direction, but the pleasant, low key atmosphere continues. The casual feeling of outdoor courtyards and verandas is set by hanging plants, natural wood and brown latticework, antiques and jade green accents. The stained glass windows came from an English pub.

Ruggles' kitchen has been expanded, and in 1977, Jachmich opened Birdwatcher's, a companion backgammon-entertainment bar. Ruggles' chef and several kitchen staffers are Korean. Chef Cheow Hwa Yong trained in American hotels in Korea.

Says Jachmich, "My food is relatively simple, but good. Decor is simple, not highbrow. We have added veal and pork to the menu, but still limit ourselves to eight or nine items; that's what most people like. Our success comes from high quality food, good prices, and ambiance. My greatest thrill is having people come back to the restaurant."

903 Westheimer

TOMATOES MANFRED

6 ripe tomatoes
6 hearts of palm
Swiss Vinaigrette Dressing (see below)

1. Slice chilled tomatoes 1/2-inch thick and arrange in layers on plate.
2. Slice hearts of palm lengthwise and place over the tomatoes.
3. Cover tomatoes with cold dressing. Garnish with parsley and lemon wedge.

SWISS VINAIGRETTE DRESSING

1/2 teaspoon Dijon mustard
3/4 cup white vinegar
1/4 teaspoon salt
1/4 teaspoon pepper
2 pinches sugar
2 cups salad oil
1 medium onion, chopped
1/4 clove garlic, finely chopped
1/2 cup chopped chives
2 tablespoons chopped red pepper
1 tablespoon fresh lemon juice
1/4 teaspoon tarragon
2 tablespoons finely chopped fresh parsley

1. In medium bowl, combine mustard, vinegar, salt, pepper and sugar.
2. Gradually add oil to the mixture, beating until smooth.
3. Add the onion, garlic, chives, red pepper, lemon juice, tarragon and parsley to the mixture. Refrigerate for at least 2 hours to blend flavors.

A successful meal must be good from the beginning to the end. My basic principles are, number one, using fresh food. We serve all fresh fish and meats. I don't buy food if I can't get it fresh, although, of course the meat is properly aged. Number two, we prepare 'à la minute'. We don't precook except for some of the sauces and soups. In order to do this, I have to have a larger staff, but I think it reflects in the quality of the food.

RUGGLES

SNAPPER FLORENTINE

3 pounds red snapper or 6 filets
3 cups water
1/2 cup white wine
1 teaspoon salt
1 teaspoon pepper
1 bay leaf
1/2 lemon
Creamed Spinach   (see below)
Mushrooms

1. Wash snapper, pat dry and arrange in a single layer in a large skillet that has a tight cover.
2. Add water, wine, salt, pepper, bay leaf and lemon. Bring to a boil.
3. Reduce heat. Simmer, covered, for about 3 minutes or until fish flakes easily with a fork.
4. Prepare spinach and mushrooms.
5. Divide the spinach mixture in even narrow strips on 6 hot plates.
6. Carefully remove fish from skillet and arrange on the spinach.
7. Top the fish with mushrooms.
8. Garnish with parsley, tomato and lemon wedge, if desired.

We recommend a California white wine for this recipe. Remember not to overcook the fish.

CREAMED SPINACH

2 (10-ounce) packages frozen chopped spinach
1/2 teaspoon salt
1/2 teaspoon pepper
1 cup heavy cream

1. In a skillet cook the spinach with salt and pepper until liquid is absorbed.
2. Add cream and remove from heat.

MUSHROOMS

3 tablespoons butter
2 cups fresh sliced mushrooms
1/2 cup chopped fresh parsley
1/4 clove garlic, finely chopped
1/2 teaspoon salt
1/2 teaspoon white pepper

1. Melt the butter in a skillet.
2. Add mushrooms, parsley, garlic, salt and pepper. Sauté quickly.

JUDY'S MUD PIE

1 cup graham cracker crumbs
2 tablespoons melted butter
2 pints coffee ice cream, softened
2 ounces Tia Maria liqueur
1/2 cup Hershey's chocolate fudge

1. Mix the graham cracker crumbs with the butter and press the mixture into an 8-inch pie pan.
2. Combine the softened ice cream with Tia Maria and fill the pie shell.
3. Freeze for at least 4 hours.
4. Just before serving, drizzle chocolate fudge over the pie.

CORDUROY MALLET FREEZE

Our version of the Velvet Hammer

Per person:

1/3 ounce Grand Marnier
1/3 ounce Kahlúa
1/3 ounce Crème de Cacao
1/3 ounce vodka
2 scoops French vanilla ice cream

1. In a blender, combine all liqueurs and vodka (1 1/3 ounces in all) with the ice cream and blend until smooth.

Tivoli Inn

Dinner for Four

Hans Christian Andersen Appetizer

*Roast Duck with Danish Style Red Cabbage,
Sugar-Browned Potatoes and Baked Apple*

Aeblekage
(Homemade Danish Applecake)

Coffee

Wine:

*With Appetizer — Piesporter Michelsberg, 1975,
or, for a drier wine, Mâcon Blanc or Beaujolais Blanc*

With Duck — Château de Lescours, 1973

With Dessert — Remy Martin or Courvoisier Cognac

Alli Harrigan, Owner

Henri Friis, Chef

TIVOLI INN

Alli Harrigan brought her native Danish cuisine to Houston in 1976 when she opened her Tivoli Inn. "For twenty-five years I had thought about owning a restaurant," says Mrs. Harrigan. "So many countries were represented in Houston but there was no Scandinavian restaurant. I wrote our menu influenced by what supplies I could get as well as what foods customers would like." All of the recipes are hers. Rich cream, whole eggs, sour cream, and butter are favorite ingredients, and special foods can be cooked on request.

"The restaurant is a costly operation because food has to be prepared right there and then. You cannot prepare it in advance. Open faced sandwiches and desserts should be made up as you serve them, and we do it that way. I have modified the big Danish or Swedish smorgasbord with the Viking Feast, which has everything from herring and seafood, meats and cheeses, to hot foods."

Tivoli Inn has a Viking ship as its symbol and its interior is keyed to the red and white Danish flag. "I decorated the restaurant as you would see it in the Scandinavian countryside." To give the remodeled building the air of a Danish country inn, she has used white stucco-textured walls, striped curtains, hanging baskets of plants, antiques, and copper pots. Posters of the Tivoli Gardens, copper etchings dating to 1740, and some of Mrs. Harrigan's own paintings that hang over the fireplace, lend atmosphere. Red table skirts with white overcloths, red and white flowers, and red napkins give the restaurant its farmhouse freshness.

Says Mrs. Harrigan, "I come from a family that is interested in cooking and that loves to have parties."

715 Hawthorne

TIVOLI INN

HANS CHRISTIAN ANDERSEN APPETIZER

Large lettuce leaves (Boston, leaf or iceberg)
8 slices fresh smoked salmon
2 hard cooked eggs
1 (3½-ounce) jar Danish Limfjord's caviar
1 (8¾-ounce) can Danish Limfjord's mussels with natural juice
8 white asparagus spears
4 cherry tomatoes
Fresh parsley

1. Arrange lettuce on four platters.
2. On each, place 2 slices smoked salmon across the middle and, to one side, half a hard-cooked egg topped with caviar.
3. On the other side arrange 12 mussels, drained.
4. Decorate each platter with cherry tomatoes, parsley and lemon boats, if desired. Serve with Danish rye or hot French bread.

A Danish meal begins with a cold appetizer. In order to serve authentic dishes here at our restaurant, it is necessary to import items such as herring and mussels.

TIVOLI INN

ROAST DUCK WITH DANISH-STYLE RED CABBAGE, SUGAR-BROWNED POTATOES AND BAKED APPLE

I use a domestic duck (Country Pride) that has the pop-up thermometer in it. *Be sure to remove all fat from inside.* I have tried all kinds of apples, but feel that the Red Delicious apples provide the best flavor. It was my father's idea to do the apples with currant jelly.

1 (4 or 5-pound) young duck
4 Red Delicious apples
8 dried pitted prunes
Salt and pepper
Water
Flour
Red currant jelly
1 small head red cabbage
Apple cider vinegar
1 cup sugar
1/4 cup dry red wine
Butter
1½ pounds tiny new potatoes or tiny canned potatoes

1. Thaw the duck, overnight, in the refrigerator. Remove all giblets, fat and neck.
2. Stuff duck with 1 apple, quartered and cored but not peeled, and 8 prunes. Salt and pepper duck on the skin only.
3. Place the duck in a roasting pan and roast at 325 or 350 degrees for about 2¾ hours to 3¼ hours, depending on weight. Add a small amount of water to the roasting pan while cooking to keep the skin from burning. When done, the skin should be crisp to the touch. This method of roasting drains fat, if any, from duck. Reserve juices and fat to prepare the sauce.
4. Skim the fat from the roasting pan, leaving only the natural juices. To them, add 1 cup warm water. Pour this mixture into a saucepan and bring to a boil. Reduce heat and add a thin flour-cold water mixture to the sauce (1 tablespoon flour to enough cold water to make a paste) to thicken it. Season with salt and pepper. Remove from heat and stir in 2 tablespoons red currant jelly.

5. Quarter and core cabbage. Dice the quarters and place them in a saucepan with 1½ cups water, plus a dash of salt. Cover pan and steam the cabbage until the water has evaporated. Add 1 peeled, shredded apple, 1 tablespoon vinegar and 1 tablespoon sugar. Simmer for a few minutes.

6. Add red wine mixed with 1 teaspoon flour. For a special touch, add 1 tablespoon red currant jelly.

7. In a skillet, melt, but do not burn, the remaining sugar with 1 teaspoon butter or margarine. Add the potatoes (drain if using canned) and sauté them in the sugar until brown. This is the last step in the entrée, but the potatoes need to sauté slowly over very low heat to prevent burning.

8. Peel and core the remaining apples and cook separately. Steam or bake the four halves until tender or done, according to taste. Fill the apples with 1 tablespoon red currant jelly. These can be cooked ahead if desired, and warmed in the oven.

9. To serve, place on each plate a quarter of the duck, some red cabbage, potatoes and a baked apple half. Spoon sauce over the duck only and serve. Garnish the plate, if desired, with a lettuce leaf under the apple and a sprig of parsley.

The Danes are very fond of pork, fresh seafood and especially chicken or duck—anything that flies. They use a lot of caraway and thyme, but the main seasoning they love is dill. In fact, I grow my own dill for the restaurant because I never could find young dill elsewhere.

You must use some imagination whether you are cooking a fish or roasting a duck. You just can't follow the book. If you want to add a spice—do it.

TIVOLI INN

AEBELKAGE

In Denmark you would have a glass of Madeira with dessert probably, but in this instance, coffee and a fine cognac will be appropriate.

10 Red Delicious apples
4 cups fine dry bread crumbs ("French bread dried in the oven is best")
1 cup sugar
1 stick (4 ounces) butter
Raspberry preserves
Whipped cream
Chopped nuts

TIVOLI INN

1. Peel and core apples. Thinly slice and cook in a small amount of water.
2. Combine the bread crumbs, sugar and butter in a large skillet and "toast" or cook until golden brown.
3. In loaf pan lined with foil, alternate layers of apples, crumb mixture and raspberry preserves, ending with the crumb mixture.
4. Bake for 1 hour at 375 degrees. Let cool to room temperature.
5. Slice and decorate with fresh whipped cream, chopped nuts and raspberry preserves.

In Denmark, food is left more natural; there is little overspicing. Danes can't eat anything without sauce, and like different sauces for different things. They always use the natural juices from the meat or seafood, and they dearly love Bearnaise sauce or Hollandaise sauce.

To cook well, try to get as much *fresh* food as possible and don't overcook.

The Poetry of French Food Houston

Dinner for Four

Vichyssoise

Breast of Capon "Nonna"

Tony's Risotto

Salad Mercedes

Soufflé Napoleon

Wine:

*With Vichyssoise — Chassagne-Montrachet
Joseph Drouhin, 1975 or 1976*

*With Capon — Château Malescot
St. Exupery Margaux, 1970*

*With Soufflé: Liebfrauenstift Kirchenstuck
Trockenbeerenauslese*

Tony Vallone, Owner

Frank Garza, Chef

"Dinner time is the most wonderful period of the day and perhaps its goal . . . the blossoming of the day." This statement from Novalis sums up Tony Vallone's approach to his restaurant. Tony's has been acclaimed nationwide and has been awarded two Mobil Four Star Awards and the Holiday Award for eight years straight. The restaurant began in 1964 and moved to its present location in 1972.

"A restaurant has a certain bounce or rhythm; it has to be orchestrated. I think a fine restaurant is a package of the kitchen for quality, the front for service, plus ambiance and timing." Emphasis at Tony's is on quality and freshness. "We feature many seasonal specialties and everything is cooked to order. I try to keep the sauces very delicate so that they don't overpower the dishes.

"As I learned, the restaurant progressed. The sauces became lighter and more delicate and the cuisine changed from Italian to French. The day a restaurant does not progress, make changes, and improve, it's on its way out. We have to cater to our clientele; we don't want them to get bored. We have as many dishes off the menu as on. Very few people even ask for a menu; they ask their captain for what they want to eat."

"We do special dinners for our wine cellar parties. For the fine wines, we bring out Baccarat and Val St. Lambert crystal. If you're going to have a great wine, you should have a great decanter and goblet to go with it."

The wines, which Tony collects as a passion, total approximately 110,000 bottles. The oldest vintage is an 1811 Lafite, but a 1790 Port is en route.

In addition to its culinary reputation, Tony's is known for special touches such as its beautiful decor, its fresh flowers and personally designed silverware. "To sum up Tony's you'd have to say that it pays attention to details."

1801 South Post Oak

VICHYSSOISE

This recipe was originated by my good friend Frank Malone. It is very important to have the cups or bowls for the Vichyssoise well chilled before using. An hour in the freezer will do the job. This will serve four to six.

2 small leeks or 4 scallions (white parts only)
1/2 medium onion, coarsely chopped
4 medium potatoes, peeled and chopped
2 cups veal or chicken stock
1 teaspoon salt
1/2 teaspoon white pepper
Pinch of cayenne pepper
4 cups cold half-and-half
1 tablespoon chopped chives

1. Combine the chopped leeks, onions, potatoes, stock and seasonings in a saucepan and bring to a boil. Reduce heat and simmer uncovered until the potatoes are tender, about 30 minutes.
2. Pour the mixture into a blender and when smooth but still a little pulpy, transfer to a large mixing bowl. Add the cold half-and-half and mix very well with a wire whisk.
3. Chill well, mixing again before serving.
4. Garnish with chives.

TONY'S

BREAST OF CAPON "NONNA"

Our fowls are true capons, flown in fresh. They're not frozen and they're not fryers. When you bite into a capon you know it's a heavier, more succulent and juicier meat than chicken. The American public slaughters fowl by overcooking it. It doesn't have to be pink on the bone, but you need to catch it just after that point so that when you cut into the meat it's lily white all the way through. It should be juicy, not dry.

4 boned breasts of capon
Lawry's seasoned salt
Ground black pepper
6 tablespoons butter
1/4 cup cognac, warmed
1 1/3 cups heavy cream
1 tablespoon meat glaze or gravy (demi-glaze or canned mushroom sauce)
2 tablespoons sherry
1 (No. 303) can whole peeled tomatoes (2 cups)
2 cloves garlic (small to medium), finely chopped
1 tablespoon chopped fresh parsley
1/4 teaspoon oregano

1. Salt and pepper the capon breasts. Sauté in a heavy skillet with 2 tablespoons butter until browned. Do not overcook; the centers should be moist.
2. Set the chicken aside, keeping it warm. Add warmed cognac to the skillet. Heat and ignite.
3. Pour in the cream and meat glaze and simmer for 5 minutes. Add sherry. Heat and pour the sauce over the chicken.
4. Discard the juice packed with the tomatoes. Chop the tomatoes and reserve the resulting fresh juice. Turn the tomatoes into a skillet with the garlic and sauté for a minute or two in remaining butter.
5. Add the parsley and oregano (just a pinch) and sauté another minute or so. Spoon a small amount of this mixture onto the center of each breast. Serve with Risotto.

The whole thing in cooking is to have a delicate touch. Don't let sauces overpower foods and don't camouflage natural tastes with spices.

TONY'S RISOTTO

For this you must use the Italian Arborio rice. It is available at food import shops. If you are making risotto for the first time you may want to add the last broth in small amounts in order not to drown the rice with excess liquid.

3 pints (6 cups) good chicken stock
4 ounces (1 stick) butter
1 medium white onion, finely chopped
1 pound Italian Arborio rice
1 cup (8 ounces) heavy red wine or Port
1/8 teaspoon powdered saffron
5 ounces grated imported Parmesan or Romano cheese

1. Bring the stock to a low simmer. You can use bouillon or canned stock if necessary.
2. In a large heavy casserole, melt 2 ounces butter over medium heat. Cook the onions until soft and golden. Add rice and stir, cooking for a minute or two, until the rice becomes opaque.
3. Add one pint simmering stock. Stir until the rice absorbs the liquid. Add the second pint. When that is absorbed, add the third pint and wine, always stirring and loosening the rice at the bottom of the pot.
4. When about half of the last liquid is absorbed, add the saffron, then the butter and cheese, little by little, stirring constantly. The risotto is done when the rice is tender, but *al dente,* ("firm to the bite"), about 20 to 25 minutes in all. When done, the risotto is creamy and bound together.

SALAD MERCEDES

I like to serve salad after the main course to prevent its interfering with the wine. For this you need firm, creamy white centered chicory or endive.

4 cups white centers of chicory
2 hard-cooked eggs
1/3 cup Italian olive oil
3 tablespoons fresh lemon juice
1/2 teaspoon seasoned salt
1/8 teaspoon ground black pepper
2 tablespoons fresh chopped parsley
1 tablespoon chopped fresh chervil or 1 teaspoon dried chervil
1½ cups julienne celery strips
1 cup julienne carrot strips
1 cup orange sections

1. Tear the chicory into small sections and place it in a salad bowl.
2. Chop the eggs finely and mix with oil, lemon juice, seasoned salt, pepper, parsley and chervil.
3. Pour the dressing over the chicory and toss lightly. Wipe the sides of the salad bowl.
4. Arrange the celery and carrots in alternating nests in a circle over the top of the chicory.
5. Place orange sections in the center.

NOTE: This will serve 4 to 6.

SOUFFLÉ NAPOLEON

Soufflés are *not* hard to do. We make soufflés of most anything. The thing that's very important is to put the egg whites in when the mixture is cool. Do not overmix the egg whites or they will break down. Fold a small amount into the cooked mixture first, then fold in the remaining beaten egg whites.

Butter
Sugar
2 tablespoons flour
1/2 cup heavy cream
3/4 cup sugar
4 large egg yolks
1 teaspoon vanilla
Pinch of salt
5 large egg whites
1/4 teaspoon cream of tartar
1/3 cup Mandarin Napoleon liqueur
Sweetened flavored whipped cream

1. Butter the sides and bottom of a 1½-quart soufflé dish generously, then sprinkle with granulated sugar. (You may need to put a foil collar around the soufflé dish to give it more height.) Set dish aside.
2. Melt 2 tablespoons butter in a 1-quart saucepan. Remove from heat and blend in the flour. Stir and cook for 1 minute to form a roux. Add the cream.

3. Reserve 1 tablespoon sugar to beat the egg whites and add the remaining sugar to the mixture. Mix well with a whisk. Stir and cook until the mixture is very thick. Remove from heat.

4. Beat the egg yolks. Beat in a little of the hot mixture, then stir in the remaining amount. Stir and cook over low heat for 1 minute. Add vanilla.

5. Transfer to a large mixing bowl and set aside.

6. Add salt to the egg whites and beat until foamy. Add the reserved sugar and cream of tartar and continue beating until the egg whites stand in small soft peaks.

7. Stir 2 tablespoons beaten egg whites into the cooked, cooled mixture. Carefully fold in the remaining egg whites.

8. Spoon the mixture into the soufflé dish gently. Pour in the Mandarin Napoleon and stir gently once or twice.

9. Place the soufflé in a preheated 375-degree oven and bake for 35 to 40 minutes. Remove from oven, top with powdered sugar and serve immediately. (The center will be a little creamy.) Serve with sweetened flavored whipped cream, chilled if desired.

APPETIZERS

Artichokes Brownstone (The Brownstone)	21
Caponatina (D'Amico's)	47
Charley's Shrimp Scampi (Charley's 517)	31
Cheese-Stuffed Zucchini (Arno's)	3
Crabmeat Maison (Rudi's)	157
French Fried Zucchini (The Great Caruso)	79
Fried Eggplant Appetizer (Ousie's Table)	141
Fried Provolone (Gaspair's)	71
Hans Christian Andersen Appetizer (Tivoli Inn)	173
Oysters Capri (Harrigan's)	87
Oysters Ruth (Foulard's)	59
Shrimp Cocktail (Hebert's Ritz)	98
Singing Shrimp (Courtlandts)	39

DESSERTS AND BREAD

Aebelkage (Tivoli Inn)	176
Apple Strudel (La Quiche)	119
Brennan's Bread Pudding (Brennan's)	16
Butter Frosting (The Rivoli)	153
Cannoli (D'Amico's)	53
Charley's Strawberries Romanoff (Charley's 517)	35
Chocolate Mousse (Maxim's)	129
Chocolate Soufflé (Foulard's)	66
Crème Brulée (Maxim's)	129
Crêpes Marnier (Harrigan's)	93
Crêpes Romanoff (Courtlandts)	43
Dante Silk Pie (The Brownstone)	26
Flan (Gaspair's)	75
Judy's Mud Pie (Ruggles)	168
Lemon Mousse (Arno's)	9
Lemon Sorbet (Foulards—served between courses)	62
Orange Slices with Grand Marnier (Hebert's Ritz)	101
Royal English Trifle (The Great Caruso)	83
Soufflé Grand Marnier (Hugo's Window Box)	108
Soufflé Napoleon (Tony's)	186
Strawberry Torte (The Rivoli)	152
Vanilla Mousse (Ousie's Table)	145
Zucchini Nut Bread (La Quiche)	118

DRESSINGS AND SAUCES

Béarnaise Sauce (The Great Caruso)	80
Blender Hollandaise Sauce (Ousie's Table)	144
Burgundy Dressing (Courtlandts)	40
Celery Seed Dressing (The Brownstone)	23
Cream Anglaise (Foulard's)	67
Esquire Dressing (Hugo's Window Box)	106
Gaspair Sauce (Gaspair's)	74
Greek Lemon Sauce (Ouisie's Table)	144
Lemon Butter Sauce (Brennan's)	15
Mustard Sauce (Foulard's)	59
Mogu (D'Amico's)	51
Old-Fashioned Sauce (Hebert's Ritz)	98
Parsley-Garlic Butter (Harrigan's)	87
Pesto Sauce (Arno's)	5
Pico de Gallo (Ninfa's)	137
Red Italian Sauce (Gaspair's)	71
Red Sauce (Ninfa's)	137
Rudi's Vinaigrette Dressing (Rudi's)	159
Sauce au Beurre Antoinette (The Great Caruso)	82
Sauce Louis (The Brownstone)	21
Sauce Meunière (Hevert's Ritz)	100
Sauce Perigourdine (The Brownstone)	25
Spinach Salad Dressing (The Rivoli)	150
Swiss Vinaigrette Dressing (Ruggles)	165
Whiskey Sauce (Brennan's)	17

DRINKS

Café La Quiche (La Quiche)	121
Corduroy Mallet Freeze (Ruggles)	169
Flying Dutchman Coffee (Hugo's Window Box)	109
Frozen Margaritas (Ninfa's)	133
Gaspair's Continental Coffee (Gaspair's)	75
Kahlúa Freeze (The Great Caruso)	83
Real Irish Coffee (Harrigan's)	92

ENTRÉES

Baked Flounder with Raisins, Pine Nuts and Almonds (Arno's)	6
Beef Wellington (The Brownstone)	24
Bracioluna (D'Amico's)	50
Breast of Capon "Nonna" (Tony's)	182
Breast of Chicken Camille (Maxim's)	128
Broccoli Quiche (La Quiche)	117
Carne Guisada (Ninfa's)	135
Chicken Calvados (The Rivoli)	151
Chili con Queso (Ninfa's)	137
Cognac Steak (La Quiche)	115
Filetto Arno Supreme (Arno's)	8
Frittata di Pomodori Verdi (D'Amico's)	52
Green Enchiladas (Ninfa's)	136
Poached Filet of Sole, Duglere (Foulard's)	61
Redfish à la Louisiana (Charley's 517)	33
Roast Duck with Danish-Style Red Cabbage, Sugar-Browned Potatoes and Baked Apple (Tivoli Inn)	174
Roast Leg of Lamb with Garlic, Rosemary and Artichokes (Ouisie's Table)	143
Roast Rack of Lamb Persille (Foulard's)	63
Shrimp in Ale Batter (The Great Caruso)	81
Snapper Florentine (Ruggles)	166
Steak with Artichokes and Sour Cream (Courtlandts)	41
Tournedos James (Charley's 517)	34
Trout Gaspair (Gaspair's)	74
Trout with Roasted Pecans (Brennan's)	14
Trout Sauté (Hebert's Ritz)	100
Veal Kottwitz (Brennan's)	15
Veal Piccata (Rudi's)	160
Veal Scallopine au Marsala (Hugo's Window Box)	107

SALADS

Brownstone Salad (The Brownstone)	23
Carrot Salad (La Quiche)	114
Cucumber Salad (Gaspair's)	73
Esquire Salad (Hugo's Window Box)	106
Green Salad Artichokes (Hebert's Ritz)	101

Guacamole Salad (Ninfa's)	134
Jill Jackson Salad (Brennan's)	14
Salad Mercedes (Tony's)	185
Spinach Salad (Courtlandts)	40
Spinach Salad (The Rivoli)	150
Stuffed Celery (Hebert's Ritz)	99
Tomatoes Camille (Maxim's)	126
Tomatoes Manfred (Ruggles)	165
Tomatoes Niçoise (Rudi's)	159

SOUPS

Avocado Soup (The Rivoli)	149
Avocado Velvet Soup (The Brownstone)	22
Basic Fish Stock (Harrigan's)	89
Cajun Gumbo (Harrigan's)	88
Chilled Cream, Foulard (Foulard's)	60
Cold Strawberry Soup (La Quiche)	113
Court Bouillon (Foulard's)	61
Cream of Broccoli Soup (Charley's 517)	32
Creole Turtle Soup au Sherry (Brennan's)	13
French Onion Soup Gratinée (Rudi's)	158
Fresh Spinach and Squash Soup with Orange (Ouisie's Table)	142
Lobster Bisque (Hugo's Window Box)	105
Minestra di Lenticchie (D'Amico's)	48
Oyster Stew (Hebert's Ritz)	97
Redfish Court Bouillon à la Louisiane (Maxim's)	125
Shrimp Bisque (Gaspair's)	72
Turtle Stock (Brennan's)	13
Vichyssoise (Tony's)	181

VEGETABLES, RICE AND PASTA

Baked Tomato (Foulard's)	64
Broccoli with Lemon Butter (Courtlandts)	42
Creamed Spinach (Ruggles)	167
Fettuccine all' Alfredo (Harrigan's)	91
Fettuccine with Pesto Sauce (Arno's)	4
Fluffy Rice Pilaf (Hugo's Window Box)	108
Fresh Jumbo Asparagus (Maxim's)	127
Mushrooms (Ruggles)	167
Potato Croquettes (Foulard's)	64
Sautéed Belgian Endive (Foulard's)	65
Spinach Soufflé (Charley's 517)	34
Steamed Broccoli (Arno's)	7
Tony's Risotto (Tony's)	184
Vermicelli with Crab and Artichokes (D'Amico's)	49

A Collection of Gourmet Recipes From the Finest Chefs in the Country!

If you enjoyed **Dining In—Houston**, additional volumes are now available:

Please send me the quantity checked:

___ Dining In—San Francisco
___ Dining In—Los Angeles
___ Dining In—Monterey Peninsula
___ Dining In—Chicago
___ Dining In—Minneapolis/St. Paul
___ Dining In—Toronto

___ Dining In—St. Louis
___ Dining In—Houston
___ Dining In—Dallas
___ Dining In—Seattle
___ Dining In—Portland

—and, available by November, 1979:

___ Dining In—Pittsburgh

TO ORDER SEND $7.95 PLUS $1.00 POSTAGE AND HANDLING FOR EACH BOOK

ORDER FORM

BILL TO

name _____
address _____
city _____ state _____ zip _____

PAYMENT ENCLOSED   CHARGE TO: Visa # _____ Exp. date _____
Master Chg. # _____ Exp. date _____
Signature _____

SHIP TO

name _____   name _____
address _____   address _____
city _____   city _____
state/zip _____   state/zip _____

Peanut Butter Publishing, Peanut Butter Towers
2733 - 4th Ave. So., Seattle, WA 98134